# How To Ruin a Great Conversation:

*How to Turn Smiles Into Frowns, Create Awkward Silences, and Not Win Friends Nor Influence People*

By Patrick King
Social Interaction and Conversation Coach at
www.PatrickKingConsulting.com

# Table of Contents

[INTRODUCTION](#) 5

[CHAPTER 1. ONLY BE INTERESTED IN YOURSELF](#) 9

[CHAPTER 2. ASK QUESTIONS NO ONE WANTS TO ANSWER](#) 19

[CHAPTER 3. OVERSHARE YOUR WHOLE LIFE STORY](#) 33

[CHAPTER 4. RECYCLE THE SAME CONVERSATION](#) 43

[CHAPTER 5. PLAY DEFENSE INSTEAD OF BEING OPEN](#) 53

[CHAPTER 6. CHOKE BEFORE THE CONVERSATION](#) 65

[CHAPTER 7. HAVE ZOMBIE CONVERSATIONS](#) 73

[CHAPTER 8. MAKE CONVERSATION A COMPETITION](#) 83

[CHAPTER 9. GO FULL CUSTOMER SERVICE MODE](#) 93

[CHAPTER 10. DRAIN PEOPLE AS A CONVERSATIONAL VAMPIRE](#) 103

[CHAPTER 11. CORRECT EVERYONE YOU MEET](#) 115

[CHAPTER 12. TREAT EVERY COMMENT LIKE A PERSONAL ATTACK](#) 125

- [CHAPTER 13. CUT PEOPLE OFF MID-SENTENCE](#) — 135
- [CHAPTER 14. DRIZZLE EVERYTHING WITH SARCASM](#) — 145
- [CHAPTER 15. BE A JUDGE JUDY](#) — 153
- [CHAPTER 16. TELL STORIES THAT ARE CONVOLUTED AND/OR TEDIOUS](#) — 165
- [CHAPTER 17. TREAT SILENCE LIKE A DISEASE](#) — 177
- [CHAPTER 18. APOLOGIZE LIKE A CORPORATE EMAIL](#) — 185
- [CHAPTER 19. OFFER PHONY EMPATHY](#) — 195
- [CHAPTER 20. COMPLIMENT SELFISHLY](#) — 205
- [CHAPTER 21. LISTEN... WITH THE INTENT TO REPLY](#) — 213
- [CHAPTER 22. RUN OUT OF THINGS TO SAY](#) — 221
- [CHAPTER 23. PRETEND TO AGREE WITH SOMEONE](#) — 233
- [CHAPTER 24. NEVER. STOP. TALKING.](#) — 243
- [CHAPTER 25. FORGET TO MAKE INTRODUCTIONS](#) — 251
- [CONCLUSION](#) — 259

Introduction

**"The great gift of conversation lies less in displaying it ourselves than in drawing it out of others."**

**Jean de la Bruyere**

Hi. It's nice to meet you. Do you want to have a conversation with me?

I'll go first. I'm curious about what made you pick up this book in the first place, and why you're reading these words right now.

Is it because you are…

- Tired of feeling awkward and uncomfortable in social situations?
- Wondering how to bring more depth and meaning to your relationships?
- Looking for quick tips on, ahem, *getting people to like you?*

Conversation is a big thing that looks like a small thing.

It's an emotional tool that helps us negotiate meaning with one another.

It's a way of thinking, creating, and learning.

It's how we know others, but it's also how we know ourselves.

Good conversation is like alchemy: inside our own minds, 2 + 2 always makes 4. But when two minds come together? It's possible to find yourself with 5. It's magical.

Conversation doesn't just reshuffle the cards. It creates new cards. It expands the deck. It gives us reasons to invent new games.

**Conversation = connection.** Every conversation is completely unique, but the desire for connection is always the same:

- We want to feel seen and heard
- We want confirmation that we are part of something bigger than ourselves
- We want to be accepted for who we really are
- We want people to really *get* us
- We want to feel like our contributions matter and have value
- We want to feel like our perspective belongs and make sense

Let's go even further with this: **We connect with others because deep down, we want the reassurance that we exist... and that that's a good thing.**

When was the last time you had a truly awful conversation?

It's probably not too hard to recall one. Thinking about it now, what went wrong? Maybe the interaction was boring, one-sided, awkward, confusing, pointless, or it just went on way, way too long…

But now a follow up question: When was the last time *you* subjected someone to an awful conversation?

Hmm. That's a little trickier.

Rotten conversations are endemic, but the embarrassing truth is that we're likely part of the problem. It's easier to identify poor conversation skills in others than in ourselves. But resist the temptation to think that you are the only sane, interesting, and intelligent person in existence, and that your mission is to simply endure other people's foibles.

Instead, our approach in this book will be to identify conversational flaws in others, and then bravely and honestly consider how we may be guilty of the same.

### **It's a Mindset Shift**

Becoming a better conversationalist is certainly a matter of learning what to *do* and *say* when you're around other people.

**But all real behavior change comes from an underlying mindset shift.** Today, conversational skills are seldom taught, but even if they were, they'd never be properly internalized without a corresponding change in attitude.

In this book, we'll learn the necessary skills, but we'll also keep returning to the deeper attitude that, in time, will make those skills natural and automatic.

Whether your goal is to make more connections, improve the connections you have, or tighten up your social skills in the workplace, this book can help.

And you've taken the first step.

The next step is to forget everything you know about communication and be open to seeing things through fresh eyes.

To be a successful communicator requires that you be *humble* and *human*. You'll only need a few things to get started:

- A willingness to learn
- A willingness to try something new
- A sense of playful curiosity
- And that's it!

If you're ready, let's jump in.

How do we ruin a perfectly good conversation? One tried and true method is...

## Chapter 1. Only Be Interested in Yourself

A magical thing happens when a mother and baby stare into one another's eyes. The baby twitches, smiles a little, and the mother responds with the same smile, only more exaggerated. The baby frowns and pouts. So does the mother.

It might not look like it, but this is a conversation.

In fact, these small, quiet moments are where every single one of us first learned to communicate. It was in these first moments that we learned that we were in the world at all, that we shared the world with other people, and that—most magical of all—those other people could be *reached*.

Through communication, we could build a bridge between our world and theirs.

A good conversation doesn't just leave you feeling seen, heard, and understood. It leaves you feeling *real*. Like you exist. Like you are not an isolated speck adrift in a disinterested universe, but a connected, valued part of something bigger and much more benign.

**Conversation is a basic human need.**

The best conversations are those that leave us feeling alive and visible:

- We have spoken, and more importantly, been heard
- Someone out there *gets* us
- We are not alone

No surprise, then, that a truly bad conversation can leave us with all the opposite feelings:

- Unheard; nobody listens when we speak
- Nobody understands us
- We are alone

The modern world is suffering from a reciprocal, self-amplifying epidemic. Most of us are desperate for more validation, care, and interest from others, yet in our attention-starved state, we are less willing than ever to validate, care for, or show interest in others. We all collectively complain that people are selfish, because they don't listen to us... yet we make no attempts to listen to them.

The biggest obstacle to real connection with a fellow human being is not stupidity or a lack of charisma.

**The cardinal sin of conversation is self-absorption.**

When you're self-absorbed, your zone of awareness shrinks down to a tiny bubble the size of your head. Inside your head, there's lots of fun stuff to do: judge the other person, jump to conclusions about them, analyze them, analyze yourself analyzing them, tell yourself stories about their intentions and motivations, and so on, round and round through all the same old neural pathways you've become accustomed to.

Inside your head, everything is already the way you like it.

There's nothing more to discover, so there's no need to ask any questions.

There's nothing to learn about the person in front of you because you've already decided who they are and what they mean, and there's no point letting an inconvenient thing like the truth get in the way of all that now, right?

You're not curious about them in the slightest.

In fact, you're not even *there* in the room with them. You're in your head. You've already assigned them a (probably not very flattering) label, and the doors of your perception are now slammed closed.

Because you're not present, you're not really listening, and you're not aware of what's actually unfolding in the encounter. You don't ask any questions; they don't answer any.

You leave the "conversation" feeling flat and empty. "Why are other people so two-dimensional?" you think. It's especially puzzling since your own inner world is so rich and complex by comparison.

Hmm.

**Conversation requires curiosity.**

Without curiosity—that is, the desire to *leave* that little bubble around your own head and go exploring—conversation is logically impossible.

However, not all curiosity is created equal:

A frog discovered by a young child may be watched with deep fascination and awe. The same frog in the hands of a scientist may find itself dissected, labeled, identified, and then tossed out once the necessary information is gathered.

*Two types of curiosity.*

*Two very different ways of connecting to the world.*

**Curiosity or *curiositas*?**

We already know that it is better to be curiously connected to the outside world than to be interested only in what happens inside our own minds.

But the desire to know, explore, and discover has both a light side and a dark side.

*Curiositas.* This shallow, corrupt form of curiosity is restless. It's not the noble call to engage meaningfully with the world, but more like the impulse to keep scrolling just to see what else may show up.

It's inquisitiveness that comes from addiction, boredom, or prying interference, and not from sincere interest and respect for the thing under scrutiny.

It's the search for more and more input, but with no regard for depth or purpose, and certainly none for the relational aspect of that information.

Basically? It's being nosy.

Asking questions doesn't reflect genuine curiosity if we ask them out of habitual politeness, or because we're going through the motions with no intention of actually listening to the answers we receive. We may seek novelty and maybe a bit of gossip, but we're not *really* interested in connection.

***Curiositas* can trap us in surface-level interactions.**

We may not even know why the conversation feels so lifeless. After all, we're asking questions, aren't we?

But if we're not present, not really listening, and not showing up in genuine ways, then those questions won't lead to any connection or intimacy. We risk becoming like the frog scientist: our approach may tick all the boxes of "understanding", but it kills the poor frog.

To counter *curiositas*, we can choose to cultivate real Curiosity Skills. According to *The Power of Curiosity: How to Have Real Conversations That Create Collaboration, Innovation and Understanding* (Taberner & Siggins, 2015) there are a few simple ways to become more present, open, and genuinely receptive.

## **Be Present to Absorb**

When we're caught up in *curiositas*, we might physically be in the room, but mentally somewhere else.

We all know it's bad to check out when someone is talking to us. Daydreaming about what we're going to have for dinner, slyly checking our phones or getting distracted by a conversation happening next to us... these things are rookie mistakes, in no small part because it will be awkward as hell to be caught out.

You can even be distracted while *within* that conversation.

If you're quietly thinking of all the things you're going to say just as soon as they shut up, you are just as distracted as if you had literally fallen asleep in front of them mid-conversation.

If you are jumping to conclusions, making assumptions, or asking questions then ignoring the responses... you're not mentally *there*.

The first step to real conversation is to be there. **Be present.**

Recognize that it's a choice to turn down your internal chatter, and to focus on them, rather than yourself.

**Be *here*, in *this* conversation, in *this* time and place, with *this* person.**

If a friend says, for example, "I just don't know if this is the right relationship for me," then just let that be for a moment. Make space for it.

See what happens when you choose *not* to immediately blurt out some trite encouragement, or ask a question because you think you should, rather than because you sincerely want to know the answer.

Try to see what it might feel like to be genuinely interested in them, their experience, and their point of view... while suspending your own.

### **Ask Open Questions**

In *curiositas*, questions can feel like weapons. They're like the scientist's dissecting scalpel, or the interrogator's bright, relentless light. **Sometimes, a question is not a question at all but a small accusation or attack in disguise.**

- "Why would you do that?"
- "What were you thinking?"
- "What's the problem now?"

True curiosity is never defensive, manipulative, or dominating. It doesn't have any goal other than sincere exploration and understanding. There is no hidden trap to catch you out, or an implied right answer that earns a reward.

True curiosity has no foregone conclusions about anything. It's not trying to give a performance of being curious, and it's not using curiosity as a shield or a tactical weapon.

It just doesn't know, and would like to know.

So, it asks open-ended questions, then makes space for the answer.

For example, instead of saying to an employee, "You're just not getting this new protocol, are you?" you can say, "I see you tried to use the new protocol this morning but had some trouble. Can you tell me about it?"

The first question is only wearing the disguise of curiosity; the second question comes from a real desire to understand.

## **Choose How to Listen**

*Curiositas* leads us to reactive listening, not true listening.

We may listen just enough to form our own response, rebuttal, or counterpoint. We listen closely, but only for little gaps where we might insert our own opinion or show that we're right about something. In other words, we're listening, but with an agenda.

**Listen to the person, and not just their words.**

Listen to understand, not to respond.

Listen to learn more about their position, rather than to push your own.

You can choose *how* to listen, and *what* to listen to.

If someone tells you, "I'm such a failure," consider that there are two different ways to hear the message they're sharing. Listen for emotional content, not just factual data.

You might respond:

"But you're not a failure. You didn't fail; you got a B minus!"

*You've listened, but to what? The data. The words.*

An alternative response:

"What makes you feel that way?"

*You've heard the deeper message being expressed here. You're listening to the person, and not just their words.*

**Be present. Ask open-ended questions. Then choose how you'll listen to the answer that you're given.**

Chapter 2. Ask Questions No One Wants to Answer

**Not all curiosity is created equal. Not all questions are, either.**

Being truly curious about the world outside of your head—and the fascinating people who live there–is great. But sincere curiosity on its own won't guarantee that you ask good questions.

Sometimes, a poor question is just a lazy question.

Sometimes, it's a careless way to waste time.

Some questions don't mean any real harm, they're just so bloated with assumptions that they don't leave much room for a real answer, and the real connection that may follow.

One of the best ways to wreck a promising conversation is to cram it full of low-quality questions that take away space that could have gone to excellent questions.

**There's an art to asking the right question.**

Questions have their own unique shape and structure; they come built in with certain assumptions and expectations, and, ultimately, they all serve quite different purposes.

Think of questions like the interchangeable bits on a screwdriver. Sure, the tool is always a screwdriver, but the exact shape of the bit on the end makes a world of difference.

A bad question is better than not asking questions at all.

But asking the right question may simply be a matter of fine-tuning—of finding the right screwdriver bit, so to speak.

Over time, you will start to recognize the telltale structure of a good question, how to use it, and when. You'll start to develop a preference for questions that are

- Open-ended
- Simple
- Unbiased
- Sincere and curious

One happy side effect of mastering this skill set is that you'll be able to field other people's bad questions with more grace and ease. According to *Find Out Anything from Anyone, Anytime: Secrets of Calculated Questioning From a Veteran Interrogator* (Pyle, Karinch & Hartley, 2014) a smart approach to inviting real dialogue is to **ask clear, efficient, and well-structured questions. Here's how:**

## **Start with a Strong Interrogative**

*"Did you do something last night?"*

Pause for a moment and consider how *you* might respond to this question. What is this question actually asking you? Well, the expectation for a yes/no response is built right into the structure of the question.

This question is literally asking for a monosyllabic response. Did you do something, yes or no?

If you ask someone a question like this, that's exactly how they'll answer. If that's not the kind of response you want, you're in trouble.

On top of this, there are all sorts of hidden assumptions about what this "something" might mean. What if I consider that all the dozens of things I did don't technically count as "something"?

If you've ever asked a child that tired old question, "Did you learn anything interesting at school today?" then you already know that you're asking for a monosyllabic response—and you know exactly which one you'll get, too. Consider instead:

"What did you do last night?"

It's the same question, with a different screwdriver bit attached. *This* one might get the job done.

As a rule, never ask a yes/no question unless you have a sadistic desire to strangle the conversation to death.

Instead, **use interrogators like**

- **Who**
- **What**
- **Where**
- **When**
- **Why**
- **How**

These will help trigger detailed, story-based responses, making dead-end yes/no responses an impossibility.

"*What* did you do at school today?"

"*Who* did you play with at break?"

"*How* did math class go?"

Interrogatives signal that you're not just trying to confirm a suspicion, you're genuinely interested in learning more. You're not just asking someone to comply with your pre-existing vision of the conversation. You're inviting them to contribute in real time to that conversation.

## **Keep the Question Short and Focused**

One way that people can feel steered in conversations is when they're forced to respond to questions that are overly long and confusing. Take a look:

"Given the difficulty of this project and the conflicting demands placed on you, do you think that you managed to meet the objectives you set, or are there some areas you're still concerned about? If so, why or why not?"

This question is, as you can plainly see, a dog's breakfast.

Pitching a question like this is not only mildly rude, but it also feels like you're conducting market research or weaseling your way through a tedious job interview. It feels intrusive, overly planned and slightly suspicious. While the person is simply trying to figure out what on earth you're asking, the conversational momentum dribbles away and any connection you had dies a slow death.

Instead, give the other person enough space to think, reflect, and freely respond to what you're asking—without feeling that you're anticipating their response.

Be clear and simple.

A good question isn't a carefully worded contract. It's just a prompt; an invitation. So, keep it short and sweet.

"How's it going with your objectives?"

### **Strip Out Biases and Hidden Agendas**

**Loaded questions are like loaded guns. They (rightly) put people on the defensive.**

When you ask a biased question, you aren't asking a question at all, but rather forcing a statement in an underhanded way. Such a question does not come from a desire for discovery, but to assert what is already felt to be known. No surprise then that the most common responses to a biased question are:

- Being guarded
- Going on the attack
- Shutting down entirely.

In worst case scenarios, loaded, forceful questions push people to lie and conceal things from you.

If you want people to be honest with you, be honest with them. If you want to be told something you genuinely didn't know before, then ask a question that makes room for that, rather than one that pushes them down some pre-conceived path.

- "So, what pet insurance do you use?" (Assumes you use pet insurance... and have a pet).
- "Why the overreaction?" (Already concluded that it is indeed an "overreaction").
- "What made you give up on such a great career?" (Value judgment: *Is* it a great career? And did you "give up" or did you bravely seek something better suited to you?).
- "When did you get over your childhood trauma?" (Uh...)

**How do we remove bias?**

If we're being honest, sometimes it means ditching the question completely ("Why are you such a stupid jerk?" is not, in fact, a sincere inquiry into someone's current state of mind).

Go back to basics. Pretend you're an alien visiting earth or a scientist or journalist trying to investigate a phenomenon in as neutral a way as possible. Play dumb. Assume you know nothing and go from there.

One of the best questions you can possibly ask: "Can you tell me more?"

## The Anatomy of a Good Question

Good conversationalists know how to ask the right questions.

According to the *New Hampshire Business Review* (Pubali Chakravorty-Campbell, 2018), a good question has the five following characteristics:

## 1. **The question should be open (CONSTRUCT)**

No yes/no questions. Make a little gesture of invitation for people to tell a *story*—not just supply a data nugget. Let people reflect and explain, in their own way. Give them the chance to unfold, not merely respond.

- "What surprised you the most about…?"
- "Tell me more about…"
- "What was it like to…?"

## 2. **The question should have RELEVANCY**

Read the room. Ask a question that fits the context, the other person, and the nature and stage of the relationship you have with them.

Curiosity is good, but it needs to be appropriately tempered by respect for time and place.

- At a work conference, ask about people's expertise and training.
- At a dinner party, ask about their relationship to the host.
- In a casual setting at the school gates, ask people about their children or holidays.

- With people you met a minute ago—the weather is your go to!

### 3. **Know what your INTENT is**

Don't ask something just for the sake of asking. Pointless questions from a place of anxiety can actually be more stressful than the awkward silences they're trying to fill up.

Be clear in yourself why you're asking questions in the first place. The gold standard is simply because you're curious and want to know, but also be aware if you're going in with a desire to learn, to snoop, to bond, to validate, to criticize, to make someone feel seen… or to make them *not* feel seen?

Be honest and be purposeful.

Drop fluff and filler questions.

Pause before speaking and decide for yourself—*what do I hope this question will do for me?*

Ask from a place of real intent and you will come across as sincere.

- "I've been dealing with something similar myself—can I ask how you're handling it?"
- "What do you think made you pursue that line of work?"

- "I'm really fascinated by your perspective on this. Can I ask you something a bit personal?"

One intentional, well-formed question is worth a million "anything planned for the weekend?" questions.

## 4. Shallow first, then deep (APPROPRIATENESS)

Don't lurch into the deep end with no warning. It will only come across as intrusive and may put people's guards up. There's nothing wrong with asking a deep or personal question… but at the right time.

Always start with a lightweight, low-stakes question and work your way up. Build comfort and trust gradually. Questions about favorite ice cream flavors may not feel particularly profound, but they're precisely what lead to the deep and meaningful connections over time, so embrace them.

## 5. Don't rush (TIMING)

On that note, understand that even the best question in the world will go down like a lead balloon if it's asked at the wrong time. Pace it. Ask a question, sit back, and let it do its work; don't let anxiety make you rush in with more questions, explanations, and paraphrasing.

Don't jump in to give *your* answer, either.

"What's your favorite ice cream flavor? Mine's chocolate, although it has to be the right kind of chocolate, and funnily enough I don't like chocolate chip, just chocolate. Mint chocolate is interesting, but…"

Just ask and make space. Silence may feel slightly more uncomfortable for the question asker, but trust that people need a little time to process.

## The Grand Unified Formula for a Perfect Question

Let's put all this together:

**A perfect question = [Intent] + [Relevancy] + [Appropriateness] + [Construct] + [Timing]**

In other words:

*In a perfect question:*

1. *State why you're asking*
2. *Pitch the topic to the context*
3. *Gauge the emotional depth*
4. *Use an open-ended question*
5. *Ask at the right time.*

To give an example:

"I've always been fascinated by people who go their own way (intent) and since we're at this art fair (relevancy) I hope it's OK to ask (appropriateness) —what exactly made you decide to pursue the creative life?"

In the real world, of course, you won't be sitting there with a formula and notepad, carefully constructing questions. This example is merely meant to give a sense of how these elements come together, and how a good question is never sloppy and random, but finely tuned and consciously chosen.

In real conversation, many of these elements will be implied rather than stated outright—but they're still there.

If you've ever used an AI chatbot, you'll have seen for yourself that **"you get out what you put in."**

Questions are not just ways to elicit specific information; they also set the tone and establish where the emotional bar is set. Large language learning models have learned from *us*, and we tend to respond to prompts much in the same way as we do. They don't tend to stop at just answering the question asked, and they pick up the tone that was inherent in the question itself, reflecting it back to us.

Ask a lazy, trite, and hollow question and that's precisely the kind of answer you'll get back.

Ask a thoughtful, interesting question and you'll get a thoughtful, interesting response.

In time, this leads to thoughtful, interesting conversations.

With a bit of luck, *that* leads to thoughtful, interesting relationships.

**Remember—it's not the answer that enlightens, but the question.**

Chapter 3. Overshare Your Whole Life Story

Today, everyone wants to be *authentic*.

We're all encouraged to be honest, be real, be raw.

Business leaders preach a doctrine of vulnerability. Speak your truth, open up... and if you do it on social media, even better. In the bad old days people bottled up their feelings and didn't express their opinions at every opportunity, and look how *they* turned out, right?

The trouble with this approach: It's a surefire way to totally tank a conversation.

Being candid about your sex life, your family drama, your existential fears, or your chronic hemorrhoid problem may *feel* cathartic—but it's foolish to pretend that it doesn't come with risks.

While emotionally guarded and stiff conversations are no fun, totally unrestrained expression can be just as bad—and far more awkward. The trouble with oversharing is that it's so hard to undo once it's done. **You can always disclose a little more, but you can never take back what's already been said.**

Oversharing arises from a fundamental misunderstanding about intimacy and the nature and purpose of self-disclosure. The truth is that oversharing is no more about closeness and intimacy than flashing a stranger in the park is akin to having a healthy love-life. Basically, oversharing is usually just the *illusion* of intimacy and connection:

Step 1: We divulge something personal.

Step 2: It feels a little risky, a little exciting.

Step 3: This heightened emotional response invigorates us. We mistake this feeling for the feeling of connection.

Step 4: We like the feeling, so we keep talking. Keep sharing. More filters come down.

Step 5: But once that buzz of faux-connection fades, we may actually find ourselves feeling embarrassed and over-exposed.

The oversharing hangover kicks in. We realize we have said things that we shouldn't have. We may have said things we don't even really think. Oops.

If two oversharers get together, they can find themselves having some truly bizarre interactions, only to slink away afterwards wondering what either of them were dreaming up.

**Why do we overshare?**

The drive to disclose may have evolutionary roots (Lowenstein and Carbone, 2023). Openly sharing personal experience may have been a way for early man to socially regulate and improve group survival. It goes without saying, however, that the social world we inhabit today is vastly more complex, and privacy and discretion are in short supply.

Why do people overshare?

Many reasons:

- Feeling nervous
- Overexcitement
- Intoxication
- People-pleasing
- Impulsivity
- Poor boundaries
- Insecurity and low self-esteem
- Loneliness
- Misunderstanding social cues
- Oversharing may even be a learned trauma response

Whatever the cause, oversharing often comes from a **sincere but misguided attempt to connect.**

It *feels* like intimacy, but it's more like emotional graffiti.

Over-disclosing often creates awkwardness and leaves everyone with a post-conversation vulnerability hangover. Instead of building a bridge, you may burn one.

Genuinely opening up to another person *is* a way to deepen trust and create a lasting bond, but this kind of self-disclosure is often a reflection of growing closeness and trust, rather than being its cause.

When personal information is blurted without respect for time and place, it doesn't feel like bonding... it feels like you just walked into someone else's therapy session.

If you're a chronic oversharer, understand that you have greater access to rapport, trust, and genuine connection if you *mutually* and *gradually* share information with another person when appropriate. The desire for closeness is legitimate... the strategy of oversharing, not so much.

### **Match the Message to the Moment**

Before spilling your guts, pause.

Ask yourself about

- the time
- the place
- the person

***Anything* can be appropriate to disclose if it's to the right person, at the right time, and in the right place**. But make that assessment *before* sticking your foot in it.

- Starting a conversation about a deep secret you've kept for years when you're rushing through the morning commute with your partner? Probably not the right time.
- Telling the guy at the supermarket checkout about your abandonment issues? Not the right person.
- Going into detail about the affair you're having while at a funeral? Not the right place.

**Here's a great test:** Ask yourself whether you would feel fine with this person repeating what you're saying to them in a room full of people.

If just the thought gives you pause, that's your sign to keep your mouth closed. Incidentally, this is also a great test to check whether you're "just concerned" or are actively engaging in full-blown gossip. Would you say *to* this person what you are now saying *about* them?

If you're ever unsure, take your cue from others and from your surrounding environment. At the very least, if you can reflect the tone and emotional depth of what's being shared with you, you're not likely to make a disproportionately intimate disclosure you'll regret later.

**<u>Learn to Sit with Silence</u>**

Oversharing can sometimes be a stress reaction.

Unfortunately, certain social conventions and assumptions about what bonding looks like can create a strange set of expectations—particularly for women. Without knowing it, we may feel pressured to reveal secrets, make emotional revelations, or share personal information because we think we have to.

But by doing so, we make connection a performance, or we slip into entertaining or amusing other people—again, not a real substitute for genuine, *reciprocal* intimacy.

We may feel that if we want those authenticity brownie points, then we have to reach for the most intense or vulnerable story we've got. Sounds strange, but it's not uncommon for some people to get trapped in a kind of authenticity one-upmanship.

If this sounds like you, try to get into the habit of really pausing.

Stop frequently during conversations to take an emotional reading and dial down the temperature.

**You don't have to be dramatic to be real.**

Take a deep breath and, instead of making a pronouncement or sharing your life story, ask about theirs. Stay in the present. "So, what's something you've been enjoying lately?"

## Filter with the Regret Test

If you walk away from a conversation thinking, "Did I say too much?" then that is a sign you probably did.

Regret is a good thing. See it as a warning sign and a prompt to regulate a little more in the direction of tact and reserve. Whatever you do, don't ignore that little voice that feels slightly embarrassed—it's telling you to tighten up your boundaries for next time… and that's nothing to be embarrassed about.

Think carefully over the conversation and see if you can identify that point at which you went a little too far. Next time, see if you can spot that point *without* crossing over it. Notice when you're getting overexcited and rein it in. One good tip—be careful if your oversharing tends to come on the heels of alcohol or caffeine and adjust accordingly.

Remember:

- Emotions can be real and valid without being broadcast
- Intensity is not a sign of truthfulness or sincerity
- It's OK to keep something of yourself back

You don't have to reveal all, and what you do reveal does not necessarily have to be revealed now, all at once. Relax and pace yourself.

**Quick trick:** Try faux disclosure. Oversharing feels good because it creates a little buzz of illusory intimacy. But guess what? You can get that same buzz without actually revealing information that will make you cringe later.

Lean in, lower your voice, and say, "Hey, can I tell you a little secret?"

And that's it.

Ninety percent of the thrill of disclosure lies in those words alone, so that it almost doesn't matter what you say next. Follow this up with the very mildest of "confessions" and you will have created the momentary thrill of a shared secret, and the fun of being invited into a secret club of two. Plus, you would have done it without making a fool of yourself.

Let's say you're at a work conference and want to get to know the person next to you better.

"Can I tell you a little secret? I'm not really a realtor at all. I just come here for the free mozzarella sticks."

## **What if *They're* the Oversharer?**

You know how you wish other people would have behaved that one time you slipped up and overshared? Behave like that!

Try to remember why people overshare: It's a misguided (and totally human) attempt to connect. Being kind in this instance looks like providing validation and recognition *without* allowing them to disclose further.

- Be warm
- Notice and reflect the emotional content you're seeing
- *Then swiftly redirect*

Don't be afraid to use a little humor:

"I know dealing with family disputes can be pretty draining, but it sounds like you're doing everything you can. (Warmth and validation) But let me stop you right there before you tell me all your secrets! We have to keep some skeletons in the closet for a rainy day, huh? (Humorous and light-hearted, but a pretty clear boundary) What

I really want to know is how your dahlias are doing this year. We've had a lot of rain, haven't we? (Tactful diversion)"

You can't always stop someone from saying something they regret, but with a little grace and kindness, you can artfully ease past it.

You can be authentic, honest, real... *and* private. You are not required to bare all and go into confessional therapy mode to enjoy someone's company or have them enjoy yours.

**Self-disclosure leads to more connection and intimacy, but only when it's reciprocal, paced, and appropriate.**

## Chapter 4. Recycle The Same Conversation

The best way to truly suck at conversations? Make sure you're never actually having any.

Instead, work out a routine and plod your way through it again and again, until you could recite the same-old same-old in your sleep.

"Hey, how's it going?"

"Yeah, we're fine. Pretty busy, but OK. You?"

"Same. Hoping the weather picks up for the weekend. You doing anything?"

"Dunno, nothing planned. You?"

"Not sure yet. Work's crazy, you know."

"Yup."

Zzzzz…

The above is a strong sign of what we can call **conversational sclerosis** (that is, the pathological hardening of the living communicative tissues that exist between people), and it's a pretty debilitating social disease that frankly needs an awareness campaign.

Sclerotic conversations:

- Are stiff and rigid; they don't flow, they aren't vibrant and alive

- Are dry and predictable; nothing juicy going on here
- Are repeats of previous conversations, sometimes almost verbatim
- Feel like chores, except you're not quite sure who is doing whom the favor

Conversational sclerosis creeps in quietly, especially in longer-term relationships of all kinds, from friendships to marriages to family connections.

What's the cure? Just wing it? Just blurt out whatever comes into your head?

Nope. Rather, we can soften and bring life to dying conversations with a little **prepared spontaneity.**

Healthy conversations are flexible and limber, but they still have some structure and shape.

They're adaptive, they contain useful information, they are fairly organized, and they don't stagnate or get stuck in any one area. **Good conversations are fresh, fluid, and *alive*.**

- They're not too limp or relaxed (like someone half asleep or on their death bed).

- They're not too rushed or stressed (like someone blasting through a battle or a punishing workout).
- Rather, they're poised gracefully somewhere in between (like a dancer or Tai Chi master).

Here are some ways to become a little more conversationally loose and limber... while still retaining a degree of self-composure and preparation.

## **Think Ahead: Prime Your Mind for Connection**

Impromptu conversations can spring up on you anywhere and at any time. But you'd be mistaken to think that there's nothing to do but rely on whatever ad hoc banter you can summon in the moment.

The word impromptu actually comes from the Latin *promptus* meaning "to be in readiness." Impromptu conversation is conversation in a state of readiness—we are open to what might unfold, but we are primed and ready with a pre-game strategy.

If you've ever observed someone responding with quick and comfortable wit in a random conversation, know this: It's not random. That person came prepared.

Think about the day or the week you have coming up ahead, and consider:

- Who you might bump into and where
- What meetings, get-togethers, and planned conversations you'll be having
- What you could potentially share with these people given the opportunity

This doesn't have to be a long or complicated process; simply run through the possibilities for encountering various people in your social network, and make sure you have a little something in the bag to pull out in the spur of the moment.

"Hi Lily, nice to see you again. Hey, how are things with your new puppy?"

"Hello, I'm James, I've just moved next door. Good to bump into you. I think I've already met your wife…?"

"Kara! Just the person I was hoping to see. I've been wondering about that blind date you had. Tell me everything; don't spare the details."

This stops you from freezing awkwardly or defaulting to lame conversation killers like, "nice weather," or "have a good weekend?" You'll feel more at ease, you'll *appear* more at ease, and the conversation will be able to move and breathe a little.

## **Have Meaningful Messages in Mind**

Planned spontaneity may seem paradoxical, but think of natural, in-the-moment expression as a kind of delicate flower that blooms best in well-prepared soil. This doesn't mean you're required to anxiously plan out verbatim scripts and lines you'll deliver at fixed times—we're trying to reduce stiffness and rigidity, after all.

Instead, take some time to identify for yourself the *broader meaning* that you want to convey in every conversation. **This is a little like giving each conversation its own branding or theme.**

- What is the emotional note you're hitting?
- What's the purpose, ultimately, of the interaction?
- How do you want to come across in a general sense?

Don't wait for a podcast invitation to talk about the things that matter to you. Don't expect that people will naturally ask you the questions that you most want to answer, or prompt you with the topics you'd most like to elaborate on. Instead, prepare a few versatile key messages you can drop naturally into conversation.

These are like soundbites that reflect who you are, what you're doing, and why. Whether you're preparing little lines or anecdotes for use at work, with your family and friends, or in your romantic life, be deliberate and proactive. If you don't do this, you wind up with the default: The stiff, awkward conversation that barely gets going in the first place, clunks along for a while, and then dies from neglect.

Spare yourself! Make sure that you feel prepared and comfortable ahead of time with some simple phrases/ideas that quickly show you in the light you want to be seen. For example:

- "I've just wrapped up an interesting project for a client and am thinking about ways to push myself even further this year."
- "Everyone talks about being a cat person or a dog person, but I never got that. Why not *both*? That's pretty much my personality in a nutshell."
- "My daughter's just started kindergarten and I don't know who cries more in the morning, me or her!"

### Collect Your Thoughts: Use a Mental Template

The way to get yourself mentally organized without a dull, pre-prepared script is to quickly structure your thoughts around a template. The structure below is easy to come to grips with once you've practiced a few times:

1. Grabber
2. Message
3. Proof points
4. Call to action (optional)

Let's take a closer look.

**Grabber**

This breaks the ice and introduces the possibility of a connection.

*"I've been meaning to ask you about this amazing pie."*

*"Is that a new shirt? Green looks really good on you."*

*"You'll never believe who I bumped into yesterday."*

**Message**

Next is the main idea you're trying to get across. This should be the most memorable part of the overall message.

*"I don't think I've ever tasted cherry pie this good before."*

*"I'm so hopeless with fashion, I need an intervention!"*

*"Remember Ted who lived next door at the house on Clarkston Road? I saw him at Starbucks!"*

**Proof Points**

Once you've shared the main message, offer a few additional details that will illustrate, support, or expand on that message.

*"I find that fresh cherries kind of lose their character when baked, but somehow yours were really flavorful."*

*"I mean, I've basically been wearing the same uniform since I was 18, you know?"*

*"I think you had a thing for Ted back then, right?"*

**Call to Action**

Finally, you invite the other person to do something: to share, to respond to what you've shared, to jump in with a nonverbal response (for example laughter), or to make plans for a later conversation.

*"What's your secret? Do you use canned cherries?"*

*"I was thinking of upgrading to a feather boa and opera length gloves. What do you think? Too subtle?"*

*"Anyway. He looked kind of single to me. Just saying..."*

The format becomes intuitive after a while.

1. **Give a little intro**
2. **Deliver the main message**
3. **Back up the main message with a detail or two**
4. **Hand over to them**

Final tip: Once you've had a quick chat (or a not-so-quick chat) with someone, make a mental note of what you said, what they said, and the overall outcome of the conversation.

This may seem like a simple thing, but you'll avoid accidentally covering old ground or asking questions they've already answered. One of the quickest ways to destroy rapport is to forget what you've been told, or default to the same tired platitudes you used last time. On the other hand, rapport skyrockets when you can show you're paying enough attention to remember the small details people have shared in prior conversations.

"Last time you mentioned you were going away over the weekend; how'd that go?"

Conversation matters too much to just fall back on the default. Stay alert, keep alive, and be ready to grab opportunities when they come.

## Chapter 5. Play Defense Instead of Being Open

It's easy to tell the difference between an argument and a conversation, right?

Right?

Or maybe not.

Most of us don't go into conversations deliberately planning to have a fight. We don't think of ourselves as difficult or aggressive people, and don't set out to be the bad guy. And yet…

If we feel threatened—even a tiny bit—we may not recognize ourselves slipping out of free-flowing curiosity and openness, and into something a lot more defensive and closed off.

"Playing defense" is, sadly, far more common than most of us realize or are willing to admit. If we feel as though others are trying to attack us in some way, we rush in to protect ourselves. Then we're no longer in conversation; we're in competition and combat.

- We close off and shut down
- We put on armor
- We take a step back
- We might even try to get a few hits of our own in before retreating

The result? The conversation shrinks and hardens.

The trouble is, we may put up our guard at the very slightest perception of threat. But what if our perception is wrong? We may have fallen into the habit of registering simple differences as threats.

**Defensiveness is the conversation killer that disguises itself as self-preservation.**

When we're on the defensive, the goal of conversation suddenly becomes control, not understanding.

The other person is not an interesting co-creator or collaborator, but an enemy to be vanquished.

We shift into wanting to prove, survive, compete... instead of to connect, relate, and understand.

Sure, playing defense keeps you safe. It also shuts us out from the thing we want, and the thing we're trying to achieve by having the conversation in the first place: *connection*.

### Stop "Enemifying"

According to Adam Kahane, co-author of *Collaborating with the Enemy: How to Work with People You Don't Agree with or Like or Trust*, enemifying is exactly what it sounds like—adopting the frame of mind where other people appear to you as enemies.

An enemy is an adversary, the cause of your problems, the one who is hurting you, and the one who needs to be fought off... and perhaps even punished.

Dramatic? Yes. But the tendency to adopt this stance towards our conversation partners doesn't have to be blatant to do damage. The *attitude* you hold to others can be entirely hidden, and yet seep out in everything you say, and the way you say it.

**Take an honest inventory. Not of your words, but of your deep-seated attitudes:**

- Do you relish online content and social media that positions others as opponents to be mercilessly destroyed?
- Do you tell yourself reassuring stories about how other people are really the cause of your problems?
- In conflicts, do you tend to grab hold of your viewpoint like a bulldog, feeling righteous and even a little heroic for being the good guy?

We all do it, and we are all encouraged to do it.

Bipartisan politics presents dialogue as an entertaining bloodsport, social media algorithms amplify and monetize the most divisive content, and the news media presents every story inside a frame of, "Who are we hating on today?"

In an increasingly polarized world, it can feel *extremely* difficult to cultivate a light, playful, and open-ended dialogue. Everywhere you turn people are going to war over all the big-ticket arguments:

- climate change
- immigration
- abortion
- religion
- racism
- gun control
- war in the middle east
- AI
- drug use
- LGBT issues

Even in a casual conversation, you never quite know when you may find yourself given pause as you realize, "Oh. So you're one of *them*."

The dumb thing about enemyfying is that it sets up self-perpetuating cycles that are hard to break out of. We sincerely find ourselves thinking, "But I'm only seeing him as an enemy because he really is! I totally get that people should be open and collaborate... but not with *this* guy. He's just wrong."

Of course, the other guy is saying precisely the same thing about you.

Again, we all do it.

What's the way out?

Pretending that the differences don't exist? Forcing agreement and consensus?

Hunting out the baddies and going to battle with them?

Many social and behavioral theorists like Adam Kahane believe that what we need is a **revamped vision of what cooperation actually looks like.**

Conversational co-creation is not the opposite of conflict and discord.

Instead, it *embraces* conflict and discord.

Big caveat here: We can never, ever, ever control what other people do, think, say, or feel. We cannot control their perspective.

We cannot change what they value or what they want.

But we have far more power than we realize to influence one another by the *way* we approach conversation—and that has little to do with the words we use or the opinions we hold.

Again, it comes down to choosing not to play defense.

Here are some practical ways to lower your shield, to appreciate and work with other people's differences, and to maintain a genuinely enjoyable connection despite disagreement. (Yes! It is possible! Even with *that* guy!)

## **Notice When You're Protecting, Not Connecting**

Keep an eye on yourself—not the other person. How are you feeling?

Be on guard for subtle signs that defensiveness is rearing its head.

- A little sudden tightness in the body, perhaps the jaw
- A sudden constriction and quickening of the breath
- A little bit more heat
- A strange little flash of fear
- A slight step or movement backwards
- A closing off or tightening of body language

When you tighten up your body, everything else tightens up, too. Your thoughts, your feelings. Even the words that come out of your mouth will be harder and spikier.

Notice if you're feeling offended—a major clue—or ever so slightly embarrassed or indignant. Notice if you've stopped listening and are now rehearsing a rebuttal or entering into a quiet little argument in your own head.

All of these signs point to one thing: You've slipped out of comfy conversation mode and gone into survival mode. The other person, even if in just a slight way, has now been enemified.

But let's pause here.

Are they *really* a threat?

We can face someone and feel:

- Dislike
- Disagreement
- Confusion
- Disgust
- Anger
- Pity
- Frustration
- Alarm
- Annoyance

All of these things are certainly unpleasant. But are they a threat? Do they actively impinge on our wellbeing at this very moment?

Are you actually unsafe when in the presence of difference?

Just try to breathe and soften your stance.

Repeat to yourself internally:

***I don't have to agree with this person to have a good conversation with them.***

Seriously. One of life's greatest pleasures is finding a genuine spark of understanding with someone who lives in a completely different world to you, with a completely different perspective.

Try it if you haven't—it's thrilling.

## Let the Moment Breathe

**No fixing. No flinching. Just listening.**

Someone is different. Someone is hard to understand. Someone disagrees with you. Someone is stupid, or foolish, or mistaken.

Someone unfairly thinks *you're* the bad guy.

And yet... so what?

It's so, so tempting to instantly react to a perceived slight and jump in to defend ourselves.

> *"That's not what I meant."*
>
> *"You don't get it."*
>
> *"You don't seriously think that?"*

But that's your armor talking, not your openness.

**Give yourself the chance to see that allowing space for other people to be what they are takes nothing away from you or your ability to be who you are.** It might sting and hurt your ego a little, but let them speak. Remind yourself that listening is not surrender, not agreement, and not condoning.

You can just rest and be respectful. You can make space and allow for differences. You don't have to have an opinion at all, and you don't have to react.

Try this: "I want to understand where you're coming from. Can you tell me a little more?"

The impulse is to spy out some snag of disagreement and pounce on it in fear. Try instead just to relax, and let it be what it is.

## Lead with Curiosity, Not Control

The little word "but" is a staple of defensive, survival mode. It's like a little barb of resistance and opposition. When it appears in conversations, you can expect friction and heat. What you can't expect is that it will do a single thing to change the other person's position or prove the superiority of your own.

Of course, you can hold any view you wish and express it as you like. **But be realistic: What do you gain by pushing against someone and their perspective?** There is no controlling other people's opinions—there's only the illusion of control. So just let it go and get back to the far more fun and enjoyable work of building real connections.

"OK, but..." is the conversational equivalent of closing a door in someone's face. The message is loud and clear: *I'm against you. We are at odds. I'm no longer willing to hear what you have to say.*

Instead, use questions to keep the door open. It is crucial to understand that this doesn't mean that you agree, just that the door is open, and that you're talking.

- *"What is it that makes you feel this way?"*
- *"Is there something I'm not understanding from your perspective?"*
- *"What do you need from me right now?"*

Curiosity turns the spotlight away from proving yourself, away from the point of disagreement, and away from framing the other person as an enemy. Instead, it reminds you to stay open and alive to the nuances of their perspective, and to the quality of the connection itself.

**It's not about winning the tug of war, it's about dropping the rope.**

You don't have to win (hint: there's nothing to win in the first place). You don't have to fight. You don't have to convince or persuade or appease or find "common ground."

Take the pressure off of yourself entirely and realize you don't have to *do* anything at all. Just explore. Be present. There is nothing for you to lose.

**Connection is more beautiful than conquest—and way more fun**. Choose a frame of openness. Even if someone is going to war, play the role of conscientious objector. Be playful.

## Chapter 6. Choke Before the Conversation

One of the best ways to destroy a conversation is to make sure it never really starts in the first place. Being "bad at small talk" is like being the athlete that trips and falls flat on their face the moment the starting gun is fired.

Maybe you would have been fine once you got going, but if you trip up right at the start, it can be difficult to recover.

You mumble, freeze, or come out with something flat or unengaging. The moment fizzles and loses all momentum. You're aware of the moment passing… and that only adds to your anxiety.

Ugh.

Awkward.

The truth is that most people don't actually like small talk; rather, they learn to *manage* it.

The beginning of a conversation often feels a little stilted and unnatural, but that's normal. It's like the first few moments of a run when your muscles are not properly warmed up yet. A little start-up discomfort is *not* a sign that you're bad at conversation, or that you're an uninteresting person. It's just that beginnings sometimes do feel this way.

Enter the ARE method, designed by communications expert Dr. Carol Fleming. This isn't a template or cheat sheet so much as the general shape that most successful small talk takes.

It stands for Anchor, Reveal, and Encourage, in that order. It's a way to structure natural, comfortable small talk in a way that doesn't require strenuous forethought or planning.

## **The Evergreen Topic**

Quick: can you think of a single topic that everyone—and I mean *everyone*—on this planet enjoys talking about?

I'm thinking of the conversation topic that will be well-received no matter when or where you mention it.

Give up?

The answer is this: The thing people love talking about most in the world is (drumroll) *themselves*.

Talking about yourself gives you a genuine neurological high. When someone is talking about themselves, not only are they enjoying themselves, but they're paradoxically enjoying *you* more, too.

The ARE method is essentially structured around this evergreen topic, but gives enough room for self-disclosure and invitations to take the conversation further—hopefully into more satisfying medium—and big-talk.

## **Anchor**

The first step is to find a way to anchor the conversation to a shared external reality. This immediately creates a feeling of connection as though, for just a brief moment, you are both part of the same "tribe."

This is easier than it sounds—**simply make a comment about the environment you're both in** and voila, you've connected to something you are both experiencing together, in real time. Opening this way helps people lower their guard and breaks the ice.

Let yourself off the hook here; there's no need for dazzling wit or an observation that will blow their socks off. In fact, Dr. Fleming calls these kinds of observations "friendly noises."

**The content doesn't matter too much. The intention is what counts**—and the intention is simply to signal a friendly desire to initiate a low-stakes interaction.

- At a wedding: "Oh gosh, here's my song! I have to admit, I never stopped being a Madonna fan."

- In class: "This has got to be the biggest textbook in the history of everything."
- At the gym: "Phew! Funny how much heavier things feel when it's hot, right?"

Not earth shattering. You're basically sending the message, "I'm noticing what you're noticing." That means you now have something in common, even if it's teeny tiny—the heat, the book, the Madonna song. There is now something to talk about.

The door is open.

### **Reveal**

To walk through that door, move onto the next step—adding yourself to the picture.

**Share something personal about yourself that somehow connects to the anchor you just dropped**. Note: *Personal does not mean intimate*. It just means that you're showing up as yourself and giving the other person a little peek into your world—which is essentially a micro-invitation for them to do the same.

You humanize yourself, you "go first", and you give shape and an emotional frame to the conversation you're trying to start up.

- "Her songs just take me back to college… which I guess is giving away my age a little!"

- "To be honest, I'm afraid even the condensed summary is intimidating me a little."
- "I've been trying to increase my one rep max for weeks now."

### **Encourage**

OK, that's the hard work done. You've laid the foundation, now it's time to hand the conversation over to them by asking a brief follow up question, connected to the anchor and the reveal.

- "Do you like Madonna?"
- "How are you finding it so far?"
- "Are you part of the CrossFit group or are you just doing your own thing?"

Just like that, you've handed over the baton—and given the other person quite a lot to work with.

It doesn't take long to move through all three steps, but in just a few moments you extend a few possible threads they can pick up and run with. They can respond to your reveal or directly answer your question.

Remember that people love to talk about themselves. By sharing a little something of yourself first, however, you keep things feeling natural, balanced, and not too forced. You may even notice that some people are naturally able to reflect the ARE formula back at you... and then you're off to the races.

## **You Don't Have to Be Interesting**

Truly, one of the things that psychs people out most when it comes to getting small talk off the ground is a simple misunderstanding of their role.

Reassure yourself:

- You don't have to be interesting
- You don't have to be charming
- You don't have to be attractive
- You don't have to be entertaining
- You don't have to be intelligent
- You don't have to be funny
- You don't have to be overly nice and sweet

All you have to do is show up, quickly take that first step, and then make *them* feel interesting. Make *them* feel charming, attractive, entertaining, intelligent, funny, and nice. Doing this is surprisingly easy and takes a lot of the pressure off. Just sit back and genuinely listen.

The rest will unfold.

Pay attention to what they say, pick up a thread in what you hear (hint: The emotional threads are usually the most interesting and fruitful ones to follow) and before you know it, the conversation will have its own flow and momentum.

Things to avoid:

- **Asking "How are you?"** It's the boiled carrots of conversation. People can be convinced to eat boiled carrots, sure, and they're not *bad*. But they're not exactly good, either.
- **Intruding on an existing conversation.** It pretty much never works. Sidle up and wait to be invited in, if you must, but interrupt at your own peril.
- **Making them do all the work.** If you merely introduce yourself or open with "hey!" you're putting the person on the spot and saddling them with the job of starting the conversation. And they could be worse at small talk than you!
- **Overtalking.** It's difficult, but try not to try too hard. Anxiety can tempt you to over-explain, to interrupt, and to overall do too much. Relax, breathe, and take the first step, then just be present. You're not performing or doing anyone a favor. Find the fun.

Small talk is just building material. Like bricks. One or two bricks don't mean much, but over time if you keep laying one on top of the other, they start to build something interesting.

**When you start with those first bricks of small talk, don't think about the houses you're going to build. Just set down the first brick and see what happens. Remember that you're not building alone!**

## Chapter 7. Have Zombie Conversations

Nobody likes a zombie conversation that should have died a long time ago but somehow just keeps going and going and going…

Charles de Gaulle thought that genius was about knowing when to stop.

If you want to become a conversational genius, then, it's not just about how you start, but how you finish.

**Conversations are a little like plane journeys—the whole flight is important, but the take-off and landing are especially important.**

Let's take this analogy a little further. Just like flying a plane, you need to *deliberately* and *consciously* orchestrate your landing, not just keep going until your fuel runs out and you crash. Take charge and be purposeful.

There is one brief, clear moment in every conversation—the moment where it would be most ideal to close off and part ways. No matter how good the conversation was or wasn't, and no matter how long it lasted, at some point this moment will come around.

Your job as an amazing conversationalist is to notice it *and respond*, or else risk all that awkwardness that inevitably comes after that moment.

You may think that continuing to talk past this moment is polite, or that you're somehow doing it for the other person. Stop! It's a trap!

Brevity is the soul of wit, and it also happens to be the secret sauce to a great conversation. Keep it short and sweet. It's best to end on a high note rather than waiting for the spark and momentum to fade, letting the conversation end with a defeated sputter.

Good endings come sooner than you think, and they're clearer and neater than you're perhaps comfortable with. Draw a clean line for your own good—the last thing you want is to leave the other person wondering, "Are we still talking... or are we just standing around now?"

If you're a person who is uncomfortable with launching a conversation, it's likely you're just as uncomfortable with bringing it to a close with tact and warmth. But ending well is good etiquette; it respects the time of everyone involved, yourself included.

## **Catch the Pause, Don't Force the Exit**

Cast your mind back to a time you felt trapped in a conversation. You kept making little ~~pleas for mercy~~ suggestions that the conversation was over, and yet the other person just breezed past them and carried on talking. And talking.

If they have an ounce of tact, people often downplay or even conceal the fact that they are ready to end the conversation, simply because they don't want to offend.

Because of this:

- We may miss the signals of others
- We need to make our own signals a little bit more obvious

Chances are, you've nodded and smiled away in a conversation you actually wish would just end already, right? Switch perspectives and realize that others have felt that way in your presence, too. I know, it's a blow to the ego.

But consider this: Sometimes *neither* person actually wants the conversation to go on, and yet politeness prevails and so the torment drags on.

Keep reminding yourself that ending a conversation is not

- an insult to the other person
- a defeat or loss
- rude or awkward

It's just one part of conversation that needs to be managed, like any other.

**Every conversation has its natural rhythm.** Rises and falls are normal, and silence is not the end of the world. However, pay close attention—some gaps of silence might be your golden cue. Are people pausing to digest and think... or is the conversational fuel beginning to run low?

If people say things like, "Anyway..." or "Well..." then take this as a definite sign to deploy the landing gear. This is the spot where you will have the safest, softest landing. No need to cut anyone off.

Other potential landing places:

- another person joins the conversation
- there is an external distraction
- the surrounding scene changes somehow

Depending on the context, you can take option 1: match their "winding down" noises and bring things to a more decisive close:

> "Yes, well, it's been really nice to chat. I've got to get going, but good luck with this afternoon... I'd love to hear about it next time!"

Or if you'd like, try option 2: use a gentle opt-in suggestion or question to gauge interest in continuing further:

"So, don't let me hold you up if you need to go... but I can chat for another 15 minutes if you're keen?"

"This has been nice. I'd probably better get back to work soon... unless you're heading that way too, and want to walk together?"

Keep things low-pressure, casual, and relaxed. Recognize the lull, gently bring it to their attention, and give them the chance to close things off in a mutual and graceful way.

## **Circle Back to the Starting Point**

Good conversations have a purpose, even if it's only small and unspoken. This is a good thing, though, because it means you can more clearly identify when the chat has done its job, and can be safely and comfortably terminated.

You can wrap things up in a natural way by referring back to this original purpose. Close the loop and gain some conversational closure. By returning to the starting point and checking the box, you make it clear to yourself and the other person that the reason for ending the talk is a neutral and reasonable one, so there's very little room for hard feelings or awkwardness.

- If you've asked for advice, for example: "Thanks so much again for your insight

on this. I'm definitely going to reach out to the management committee and see if I can organize a meeting."
- If you've attempted to glean information or get an update on something: "OK, I'm all caught up now, I'll make a note in the file."
- If you've simply wanted to connect emotionally and gain a little reassurance: "I feel a lot better now. It's great to touch base, thank you."

All of these are essentially code for "The box is ticked. It's OK to move on."

Of course, for this to work, you need to have some pre-existing idea of the purpose and function of the conversation—and it needs to align with *their* understanding, too.

Use a little nonverbal communication and body language to boost the message:

- Stand up if you've been sitting
- Lightly tap your thighs, or clap your hands together
- Display a little more energy in your posture—sit up straight, take a deep breath or sigh, or shift position
- Make little leaving gestures—putting on a coat, picking up a bag, grabbing keys, or drifting towards the door

## **Make Your Exit Task-Focused, Not Personal**

It may sound silly, but ending a conversation can trigger some strange and quite irrational feelings—even if they're only mild or completely unconscious. If you've bonded well and created a precious little moment of connection and warmth, it can almost feel like a mini trauma to break that.

Try to remember, however, that goodbyes in and of themselves are not actually stressful; rather, it's all the implied baggage we saddle them with.

- Ending a conversation doesn't mean that the conversation has failed, or that anyone is rejecting anyone else.
- Ending a conversation doesn't mean that there's a problem, or that something unpleasant or awkward has happened.
- Basically, ending a conversation *doesn't mean anything*.

If you get caught up in the emotional baggage of goodbyes, you can wind up making things worse. By forcing some obviously made-up excuses, you make things more awkward. You may find yourself ultimately being blunter and more impolite than you would have needed to be if you had simply ended things earlier.

Take the emotion out of it. It's not personal.

Use a straightforward (and honest!) exit line and be clear and warm. Do not focus on what you're ending, but what you're doing next—this is just signaling a new shift in your attention or priorities.

- "Well, I've got a big project due tomorrow, so I'm going to hop to it!"
- "I just needed to say a few quick words to the host before I leave—but it was so nice catching up."
- "I need to head out if I'm going to avoid traffic, but let's catch up again soon."

Note the use of the word **need**. It's about you and the task, not about them or the conversation you've just had. There's no need for theatrics about how much you wish you could continue talking but can't (this can backfire!). Instead, keep things neutral, brief, and friendly (a smile helps) and then, whatever you do, *don't continue the conversation anyway*.

The truth is that most people are more than willing to heed a clear signal and gracefully step back.

But what if they aren't?

Send another, clearer signal. You can gradually increase the obviousness of the signal if they're not getting it. Try:

- "Is there anything else I can help you with/anything else you needed?"
- "This was a nice chat. I've got to get going, take care!" (notice the framing of the conversation in past tense).
- "OK, lovely to see you. Goodbye now." (yes, you're allowed to just say goodbye).

Try always to end with appreciation to reinforce the success of the conversation. Thank people, verbally acknowledge that you've enjoyed talking with them, and, if you like, make a few noises about what you might do in future. Smile.

**Be brief, be assertive, and be nice.**

**Land the plane safely and smoothly (and quickly) with a little fuel left in the tank.**

## Chapter 8. Make Conversation a Competition

You: "I don't know, I've been a bit down lately. Work's crazy, and I'm just feeling so done with it all."

Them: "Man, join the club. I've battled depression for years. But you have *got* to push through. Do you meditate? Check your diet as well. Once I wised up and cut out gluten, my mood instantly improved."

Are you as annoyed by this exchange as I am?

Let's take a closer look. What is implied by this person's response?

- You're feeling down—but they've *battled depression*.
- You're feeling done with it all and frustrated, but they already know all the answers and will teach you.
- You spoke up about your feelings—but now you're talking about theirs.

Sigh.

The spirit of competition in conversation is not just about "one-upping" a person. It's the deeper tendency to keep a kind of mental scorecard, or to constantly position yourself as somehow superior: You already know everything they're saying, you have all the answers, and what's more, your experience with this topic is just bigger and somehow more legitimate.

If you want to know just how devastating such an attitude can be, re-read the exchange above and consider how you feel like responding. There's not much to say, right? **Connection fizzles when people are made to feel like conversation is a contest… and they're the losers**.

Resist the urge to raise the bar or make comparisons—even subtle ones.

Competitive language is *everywhere*, and you may not even realize you're using it. For example:

- Framing people's emotions as weaknesses, confessions, or something unfortunate to overcome.
- Putting people's accomplishments alongside your own and trying to one-up them.
- Putting yourself in the position of arbiter, i.e., the wise one in the interaction who can explain everything and say what it means.

The spirit of competition creeps in even when we don't have those intentions. We may want to help with advice, motivate people, or share something of ourselves.

Competition is most insidious, though, when it pretends to be empathy.

- "Losing a parent is hard, I know. Try losing both before the age of ten, like I did."
- "How can you complain about being fat? You're healthy, be grateful for that. There are people out there who would give anything for a normal, healthy body, just remember that."
- "Everyone's usually super overprotective about their first child. Trust me, by the second or third, that wears off!"

Underneath the pretend empathy is a hidden message: "You're behind. Catch up."

Instead, be extra alert to this dynamic and try to shift out of it. You want connection, not comparison, not competition.

**Be with people where they are.** Resist the temptation to imply that they should be somewhere else (i.e., where *you* are).

## Name Experiences Without Evaluating Them

Whenever someone starts to talk about their feelings, their failures, or their accomplishments, take this as a sign to pause. Notice any impulse to jump in and somehow claim what they're sharing. It's not what you say but the intention beneath it:

- "Tell me about it! I had the same problem… but worse."
- "I did it faster / I found it easier / I got there before you / my suffering was greater."
- "I figured this out. You can too. Or at least, you should."

The thing is, you don't need to be any kind of authority on their experience to just name it. Witness what's being shared without trying to rank or force your own interpretation. Their experience can just stand as it is—without you needing to lift yourself above it, or lower yourself beneath it. (Hint: You don't even need to be in the picture in the first place)

- Competitive: "*I* got over my depression by cutting out gluten and meditating."
- Connected: "Wow, that sounds hard. I've had moments like that, too."


- Competitive: "It's called demand avoidance, look it up."
- Connected: "What do you think is making you feel this way?"

- Competitive: "You graduated? Me too. Two years ago, already."
- Connected: "Oh congrats! Do you think you'll do anything to celebrate?"

Listening with the intention to connect does not mean you go into doormat therapist mode (more on that later) or that you play small. It's just about making enough space for other people and the messages they're sharing. It's about having enough respect to give people a place to be proud, to be upset, and everything in between—without needing to somehow link their experience to ours.

## **Bring Back the Context**

Competitive language flattens out people's experiences. It turns the living, breathing soul of their message into dead data. When we're listening with a competitive spirit, we reduce people to their experiences, and forget the *person* underneath all that, the human being having those experiences.

When someone says something, we may hear the words and experience a little ping of recognition. "Aha, depression, I know about that."

It takes real presence of mind to pull yourself away from your own assumptions and expectations and reconnect to the real person in front of you, and the real story they're telling you.

You may "know" all the words they're using, and the emotions they're pointing towards. But you don't know *their story*. To learn anything about that, you need to really listen.

Ground the conversation in real life, here and now.

Ask questions. Seek more context. The more context you have, the richer and deeper your empathy. **Experiences are not the same as facts about those experiences. People's feelings are not words.**

- Competitive: "You can't take things so personally. Trust me, I've had way worse breakups."
- Connected: "Jeez, the whole thing sounds awful. How are you feeling about it all now?"


- Competitive: "You have to put yourself out there. That's how I got my first client."
- Connected: "You're making so much progress! Any ideas about what's next?"

- Competitive: "Pretty much every new mom goes through it, it's normal."
- Connected: "So, sleep training. Tell me more. How are you coping?"

When you're in compare and contrast mode, when you give thoughtless advice or one-up the person, you're cutting the experience down to size and telling it what it is.

Instead, make space and invite that experience to unfold in the way it wants to. Ask it a question.

**Instead of, "You're X" ask it, "What are you? What's that like?"**

## Respond to Connect, Not to Compete

What causes us to speak with the spirit of competition?

Most often, a misjudged attempt to relate. If we're clumsy in our effort to show that we understand, we may end up overshadowing and accidentally redirect the spotlight to ourselves, our experiences, and our interpretations of things.

But you can connect without centering yourself.

You can help and support without fixing.

You can share without one-upmanship.

Any response you make can do one of two things:

- Sustain attention and focus on the speaker, or
- Shift that attention and focus away from them (i.e., onto you)

Granted, conversations should be fair and balanced. But most of us could do more to hold space for others to fully express themselves and unfold their message—without trying to pull the focus back to ourselves.

No need to jump in and make an appraisal, say what we think of their message, or check how it measures up. Instead:

- *Ask questions* instead of making statements.
- *Reflect and paraphrase* instead of assigning labels and judgments.
- *Give space* instead of taking it up.

Ultimately, the golden rule of conversation (which we'll return to again and again in this book) is to **choose to prioritize connection** over just about everything else.

Choose connection over being right, over being the winner, and over being the authority.

See things from their point of view. Do you want people to leave conversations with you feeling heard—or *judged*?

**"The true spirit of conversation consists in building on another man's observation, not overturning it."—Edward G. Bulwer-Lytton**

## Chapter 9. Go Full Customer Service Mode

Pop quiz: What do you believe your role is in a conversation?

a) To guide
b) To solve problems
c) To analyze
d) To lecture
e) All of the above (plus a little scolding if necessary)

Sometimes we don't even notice when we're slipping into a kind of parent/child dynamic in conversations.

We may mistakenly think that our role is to be a kind of fixer. We're wearing little customer service headsets and troubleshooting... even though nobody asked us to.

It's a common error to make, but we need to consistently remember that someone sharing their feelings with us is not acknowledging our superior position. **Asking to be heard and supported is not the same as asking for advice.**

Unsolicited advice almost always feels like a teeny tiny criticism, no matter how good a place it comes from. We may think we're helping, but if we launch into fix-up mode, the actual message we're sending is:

- You're doing it wrong.
- Your efforts are insufficient.
- You didn't think this through.
- Your judgment is poor.
- You've made a mistake.

By introducing this dynamic, you risk making people feel misunderstood or judged. If someone just wants to vent or reflect, you may even end up offending them by offering up rather obvious solutions that are beside the point.

"Customer service mode" may be well-intentioned, but it still sucks. Here's how to *listen* to other people's problems without needing to find solutions on their behalf.

### **Bite Your Advice Tongue**

Notice the urge, then choose to repress it. Even just for 30 seconds.

The solution may seem so obvious, and so clear to you. But remind yourself of something: **They don't *want* your solution**. Not even a little bit.

What they really want is:

- To talk
- To think aloud
- To a little
- To vent

- To express

So give that to them. Give them space to talk and leave any silences open. Nod. Wait to see if they have something more to say. An amazing thing can happen when people are just left to talk: They often arrive at the solution themselves, in their own time.

If you keep interrupting with your solid gold lifechanging advice, you'll delay that process.

Your friend says, "I'm so tired of my job. I feel stuck."

Wrong move: "Then quit! Find something more your style."

Right move: Nod. Bite your tongue for 30 seconds.

They carry on for a few more minutes.

"I don't know" they eventually say. "I guess I'm worried of taking the leap and finding there's nothing out there."

And there it is. The conversation is moving along in a productive direction without you hovering over it with a repair kit.

### **React Like a Friend, Not a Therapist**

I know a few people who think they're good with people.

They're "psychologically literate" and consider themselves a notch above average when it comes to empathetic communication. They're smart, they're kind, and they've done a basic counselling skills course at their job.

And they're *terrible* conversationalists.

Today, therapy-speak is ubiquitous and most of us know that life is much better when we're compassionate and listen well. We know we need to recognize and honor the emotional element, which has traditionally been ignored or downplayed.

That said, we should never model our conversations on the kind of therapeutic dialogue that happens between a professional and a paying client.

**Taking on the role of unpaid therapist brings all sorts of complicated (and mostly useless) dynamics into a conversation that should preferably play out as an *equal co-creation*.**

You can listen without therapy jargon, and you can understand without reaching for the nearest lay diagnosis. Just be a friend, alongside another friend.

- Accurately putting a name on someone's experience or emotion: good.

- Launching into full-on psychiatric diagnosis: less good.

If someone's venting about a tricky relationship situation, don't go in with, "Maybe you need to firm up your boundaries. He's got an insecure attachment style and is clearly not emotionally available."

Instead, let them know that you're there with them—not above them, and not detached, either, watching from afar wearing Sigmund Freud glasses.

"Wow, I'm so surprised to hear that. Where do you think this is coming from?"

When you rush in to make a performance of being a compassionate, active listener... you actually stop listening. When you get bogged down with clever-sounding labels and theories, you lose connection with the real situation unfolding before your eyes.

## Offer a Choice, Not a Lecture

**Sometimes people do want advice—but they want to ask for it.**

You might determine that someone needs your advice, but that means nothing until they've come to that conclusion themselves.

It's not exactly listening vs. giving advice. Some people will want something somewhere in the middle. A good conversation can be a way to help people think through things and work their way up to the solutions they already know are there.

**One easy way forward: Just ask.**

"I've got a few thoughts about this if you're open to them, but if you just want to unload, I'm here for that, too."

You're not giving advice but asking them if they want you to give it. They can decline without feeling rude—plus, they'll trust you more for respecting that line.

**Another easy trick: Don't frame it as advice at all.** Ask, "Hey, can I make an observation?"

*Then wait.* Notice their reaction. If they seem genuinely ready to hear your take on things, then go in gently with your perspective, without making that advice seem written in stone. Don't lecture or make pronouncements.

"I've noticed that you often seem really upset after spending a weekend with him. Have you noticed that, too?"

If your offer of advice doesn't get much of a reaction, that's OK too. Hang back for the time being. You might feel a little annoyed that they aren't desperate to hear your sage wisdom, but consider that unless they're truly receptive to it, your advice will make no difference anyway, whether you say it out loud or not.

## **A Word on Phrasing**

When people are struggling with a problem, they're vulnerable. Something is wrong in their world, and they may feel confused, angry, sad, or powerless. It's an uncomfortable position, and it can be difficult to let other people see you in that discomfort.

If someone has taken the risk of opening up to you—even just a little—respect the position they're in and take care of the trust they're put in you. Too many of us experience a kind of emotional schadenfreude, i.e., just a little too much glee at hearing the details of someone else's misfortune. It's a nasty but all-too-common habit.

If you're in the position to give solicited advice, do so in a way that cannot be felt as criticism or judgment:

So that they don't hear, "You're doing it wrong," make a point of highlighting what they've done right so far. Acknowledge their strength.

> *"It's great that you're asking these questions."*

So that they don't hear, "Your efforts are insufficient," try to reinforce that they have their own ample resources to draw on, and *can* find a way out.

> *"You've faced issues like this before and I know you'll figure it out, one way or another."*

So that they don't hear, "You didn't think this through," try to normalize the problem and take shame and blame out of it.

> *"Nobody could have prevented this happening. It's not your fault."*

So that they don't hear, "Your judgment is poor," continually involve them in the problem-solving process.

> *"What do you think about trying XYZ?"*

So that they don't hear, "You've made a mistake," emphasize that the problem is solvable, that nothing is permanent, and that there are always options.

> *"Let's find a way through this."*

Even if you don't give any practical advice about how to solve the problem at hand, phrases like the above will help show that you're genuinely listening and offering support.

Advice has value. But being listened to, respected, and supported is usually far more valuable, and far more desired.

**When you counsel someone, be gracious and tread lightly. Make it seem like you're just reminding them of something they've forgotten, rather than showing them something they are unable to see.**

# Chapter 10. Drain People as a Conversational Vampire

Conversation is about what you say.

But it's also about how you show up.

Try watching a scene in a movie where two characters are having a dialogue or interaction, but mute the sound. Tune out the words entirely and focus only on body language and facial expression. If you watch something in a foreign language, then you can also listen closely to the volume, pitch, and quality of the voice itself, without getting distracted by the words.

You'll notice something instantly: **Conversations are all about energy exchange.**

When we turn up to a conversation, we're bringing baggage:

- Our expectations and past experiences
- Our personality and unique perspective on life
- Our opinions, interpretations, and contributions
- And perhaps most importantly, we're bringing our *vibe*

You know what it's like when you share something exciting with someone and they respond to you with all the vigor of a stale piece of toast? They may make all the right noises but the way they do it just deflates you somehow.

That's deadfish energy.

It's low, flat... and kind of dry.

In the presence of this kind of energy, you may feel like you're oversharing, like you're trying too hard, or somehow missing cues. The crummy power of deadfish energy is to make all the surrounding vitality feel like it's "too much."

People who stress over "I don't know what to say in conversations" might find it more useful to think about the social energy they're putting out—because the literal words don't matter as much as they think they do.

Your social energy is not an on/off switch. Rather, you're *always* putting something out there in the world, whether you're conscious of it or not. There's no such thing as neutral or no energy.

Ever leave a conversation feeling such a buzz that you literally couldn't sleep that night?

Or maybe a certain conversation has been such hard work that you almost feel hungover afterwards?

It's not about the content of these conversations (although of course this matters), but rather about the energy exchange. It's give and take.

- ***Good conversations*** have free-flowing energy exchange that leaves both parties with a little more sparkle than they went in with.
- ***Bad conversations*** are the opposite. Energy flows one way, depleting one party, or it flows straight out of the conversation entirely, leaving both feeling drained and exhausted.

Again, it's not only about the content of the conversation, but the emotional energy that flows alongside it. You could talk about a nice, interesting topic in a totally exhausting way, and you could also talk about a really serious and difficult topic in a way that leaves you feeling light and refreshed.

**In any encounter, you are either giving energy, taking energy, or losing energy.**

People newly in love? They give so much energy to one another they both seem to buzz and shine.

People in a fight? The "winner" is really the one who has (forcibly) taken energy, and the loser has lost that energy. The loser may in fact be handing that energy over in guilt, despair, exhaustion, or resentment. They are unable to let go of that energy-sapping connection, and it bleeds them dry.

People stuck in dull conversation? It's not like the fight, but energy is going somewhere, and most likely both parties turned up with little, gave nothing, and the chore of keeping the interaction going drained away what little there was.

Let's break it all down according to two main factors—energy level (high or low), and energy quality (positive or negative):

- **High Positive Energy** – Warm, engaging, lively. This is the energy of an excited friend, a puppy, a motivational speaker, or someone conveying amusing or happy news.

- **High Negative Energy** – Intense, reactive, confronting. This is the energy of someone ranting, defending themselves, or making an impassioned plea.

- **Low Positive Energy** – Relaxed, grounded, reflective. This is the calm energy of a napping cat, a good listener, or a wise priest offering gentle suggestions.

- **Low Negative Energy** – Lifeless, flat, disengaged. No eye contact. It's unresponsive and bored. Limp vibes all around. This is deadfish.

The thing is, there's a place and time for all of these variations—but deadfish mode is the one most likely to zap away any existing energy and kill the entire conversation, not to mention tank everyone else's mood.

While being *actively* negative is usually no picnic either, it still brings energy and movement into the conversation, which has value. This is why you can often jump start a flagging conversation by saying something a little controversial or unexpected—people may be taken aback, but now they're sitting up and paying attention. That little zap of energy has got things moving again.

Break down good humor into its constituent parts and you will discover that much of the zing and playfulness actually comes from this kind of edge. Masterful comedians know that positive or negative doesn't always matter—what matters is that jolt of playfulness a good joke brings.

On the other hand, deadfish energy, even if accidental or unavoidable, makes people feel unimportant. Nothing is more disappointing and exhausting than the realization that your conversation partner is not thrilled by your presence, your contribution, or the dialogue you are co-creating. Nobody wants to drag, and nobody wants to be a drag.

Here are some ways to be more mindful of conversational energy—yours and others'—and how to become masterful at regulating it.

## **Plug Yourself in First—Before You Speak, Charge Your Spark**

You wouldn't go on a road trip without filling the tank first, so don't enter into conversations with nothing in your social reserves. Don't rely on others to supply that energy for you.

Before any interaction, just pause and gather yourself. Take a quick reading on where you are, energy-wise. Take a deep breath, stretch, or even splash some water on your face. Reset yourself.

Real life social obligations don't always accommodate our own energy rhythms. Realistically speaking, you may not have the energy needed for every conversation. Thankfully, there's a lot you can do to make sure that on balance you're a conversational *giver* rather than a *taker*:

- Ask yourself if there's anything you're *genuinely* curious to know or learn about this person. Real curiosity always brings energy and it is way more fun than plodding through a question set you don't actually care about. When you don't make things a chore, you'll miraculously find energy for them. Find the fun.

- Avoid starting conversations by expressing how tired, busy, or stressed you are. It's a heavy tone to set and it tends to squash the conversation before it even starts.
- High, positive energy doesn't mean bouncing off the walls or being a comedian. Even if you're not 100% feeling it, signal that you're awake and engaged in small ways. Ask questions that focus on hope, excitement, novelty, intrigue, or light humor.

Everyone's social battery runs flat now and again. If yours is truly run-down, do what you can to avoid demanding social interactions till you get your spark back. Things can grind down into full-blown hostility and conflict if both parties are showing up with empty tanks. Avoid this by recharging first.

## **Shift from "Take" to "Give" —Feed the Moment, Don't Just Feed off of It**

There's plenty of talk today about introversion and extroversion, i.e., how some people are drained by socializing, while others are energized by it. The truth may be a little more complex than this.

**Most of us move between the roles of giver and taker.** There may be individual preferences and long-term patterns in relationships, but remember that every interaction is unique. Every conversation is a new encounter.

Think in terms of energy flow in the here and now.

Outgoing people are said to gain energy from social interaction, but often they're the ones bringing the most energy, too. They may be doing most of the heavy lifting when it comes to keeping the conversation alive, fresh, and moving, while others sit back and take it all in, contributing little.

On the other hand, shy and introverted people may say little and keep a low profile, yet emerge from socializing feeling overdrawn because they have been tirelessly feeding the conversation with enormous empathy, attention, and listening.

It's not about introversion or extroversion, and it's not about how much someone is talking or what they're talking about.

It's also important to pay attention to the kind of energy you're bringing..

- Don't treat conversations as a dumping ground.
- Don't vent and overshare under the guise of being open and communicative.
- Don't expect others to carry you.

These things definitely bring energy, but it's not the good kind.

Think carefully about what kind of energy you are bringing and be more deliberate.

Can you bring interest, encouragement, validation, warmth, or attention?

Can you bring a calm or sunny disposition to the table?

Can you hold a frame of lightness and ease?

Aim to keep a 2:1 ratio—for every story or anecdote you share, ask two questions.

Constantly be aware of whether you are a giver or taker—remember that talking isn't necessarily giving. Are you adding to the conversation or just greedily taking what you can from it and leaving others to pick up the slack?

## Notice the Loop—Be Here or Be a Drain

Think of a conversation like a delicate red balloon that two people take turns bouncing back and forth, working together to keep it afloat. If someone gets distracted or neglects to take their turn, the balloon can quickly fall to the ground and maybe even pop.

Energy leaks happen when the mind is distracted and pulled elsewhere. You're suddenly thinking of yesterday's balloon game, or thinking ahead to how this balloon game ends, then all of a sudden, you're zoned out. When someone checks out of conversation, others notice. That's an energy leak.

Here's the thing, though: Normal conversations have some wiggle room. You don't have to show up with laser-like focus 100% of the time, and it's normal for your mind to wander off now and then.

If you do catch yourself drifting, just gently come back. Find a way to reconnect to the flow by asking a question, paraphrasing what you've heard, or reaffirming your presence and interest.

- "So, let me just see if I understand you, you're saying..."
- "Hang on a second, could you please just repeat that last part?"
- "Im sorry, I zoned out a bit there! You were saying that..."

Sometimes you're going to miss a beat and let the balloon touch the floor. That's OK. Conversations can recover and continue when you reconnect with grace. You just have to show the other person that you're present, and that you have some energy to contribute to kick things off again. It's a little like catching the balloon just before it's about to hit the ground.

**Don't enter interactions tired and depleted.**

**Don't passively feed off of an interaction without contributing.**

**Don't zone out and let energy leak away.**

## Chapter 11. Correct Everyone You Meet

An old urban legend describes how Queen Victoria hosted a foreign dinner guest one day, and at the end of the meal, finger bowls filled with lemon water were served to the guests. The oblivious guest proceeded to drink from the bowl, instead of washing his hands in it. Rather than correct him and cause embarrassment, however, Queen Victoria is said to have quickly sipped from her own finger bowl, and at once all the other guests followed suit.

Now, this story is probably not true, but then again, a focus on meaning rather than raw accuracy is precisely what this story is all about…

The Queen showed true tact and decorum not because she knew what the "right" thing to do was, but rather because she was wise enough to put her guest's comfort above her need to win.

It's the same in conversation.

**True fact: Nobody really cares if you're right.**

Think about the people you most enjoy talking to. Those people you consider likeable, charming, and excellent conversationalists.

What exactly is it about them that makes their conversation so enjoyable?

- "I just love that Sam always knows the right answer."
- "Lee is great fun. His facts are always perfectly accurate."
- "I like talking to Sasha because she always helps me understand what mistakes I'm making."

You get where this is going.

Being the "well, actually," personality may be fun for the one doing it, but it's tedious for the victims.

Some people are conversational jocks and want to turn dialogue into a contact sport. But others are conversational nerds and want to turn every innocent discussion into a kind of gameshow quiz.

Correcting others is one of those tiny but damaging habits that can happen without us even knowing it. It's simple; we hear someone give an incorrect date, muddle up a story detail, or mispronounce a name, and we automatically jump in to put it right for them.

There are ways to correct people with tact and care, but the truth is that most corrections are *not necessary in the first place*, and they tend to replace connection with discomfort.

You may feel you are being helpful, but for the other person, it can come across as condescension. Even if you're right, the correction acts like a speed bump in the middle of the conversational flow. It may feel rude, a little nitpicky, and almost like a mild power play—even if it genuinely isn't.

If you're a chronic corrector, you may very quickly chip away at people's trust, making them feel guarded when talking to you.

**Usually, the purpose of conversation is connection, and not precise data transfer.**

That means that when we get hung up on details, we risk breaking connection to make a point that never really needed to be made.

Does this mean we should never correct people? Of course not.

In certain contexts, conversation will be more focused on accuracy and truth, and a polite correction may be necessary to prevent misunderstanding.

Nobody would take offense at us correcting the spelling of our name, for example.

The main thing is that our *priority* should always be the strength of the connection; even if we correct someone, we do it without damaging rapport.

It's fair to say that most corrections don't fall into this category. Correcting someone's grammar, for example, may provide a little thrill of self-righteousness, but the person being corrected is less likely to remember your "lesson" and more likely to remember the embarrassment they felt in receiving it, unsolicited.

The "I was only trying to help" defense may not hold if deep down, we're just doing it to assert dominance or make a point about our (slightly) superior position.

Correction, if you simply must do it, should be offered with empathy, honest intentions, and with respect for context.

**Ask yourself which is more important: perfection or communication?**

### Correct Privately Whenever Possible

Correcting people in public carries extra complications and should almost always be avoided. No matter how sincere your intention to help, it will be overshadowed by the other person's humiliation.

- Is the correction really **urgent**? Is it essential that the correction happen immediately, right now?

Is the correction super **important**? Is it life or death that you chip in right here, right now?

If you can, either drop the issue entirely or wait and talk to the person privately later.

"Hey, just wanted to mention—at the meeting yesterday, the guy seated to your left is actually *Austrian*, not Australian. I figured you'd like a heads up just in case!"

Be discreet, be dignified, and keep it short and sweet.

You'll come across as supportive instead of critical if you frame the thing as, "Oopsie, there appears to be a mistake. But there we go, it's fixed now. Moving on…"

Focus on the correct thing, not on the mistake, and especially not on the fact that *they* were the ones to make it. You don't want to convey the message, "I can't believe you got that wrong," but rather something like, "Oh, an unexpected accident. Never mind, here's the right thing. That fits you better."

## **Soften Your Language and Tone**

"Actually…"

"No."

"That's wrong."

It's not the fact that you correct someone, but *how* you correct them.

You can make your point perfectly clear without using divisive, confrontational, or negative language. Instead, choose language that makes you seem flexible and cooperative. There are endless ways to frame a correction so that it goes down well:

- **A shared memory:** "Is that how long ago it was? I could have sworn I remember Annie being with us, so it can't have been more than a year ago."
- **An observation:** "I've only heard that word pronounced *cash* and never *cash-ay*. I wonder if it's a regional thing."
- **A gentle suggestion:** "I'm not sure about this but you might want to double check those prices, I have a feeling it's gone up since."
- **A shared mix-up:** "Oh man, I always get confused about this too. I think *28 Days* is the rom-com with Sandra Bullock, but *28 Days Later* is the horror film."
- **A casual question:** "Does *fanny* mean something different in the UK than it does in America?" (Hint: It sure does.)

**Frame the correction as a non-threatening, shared learning experience,** not a rebuke or a gotcha moment. Try not to stop up the conversation and get back to the flow of things as quickly as possible.

## **Ask Yourself: "Does This Really Need to Be Corrected?"**

Initially, it may feel of utmost burning importance that you say your bit.

But let's dig a little deeper. What's the emotional payoff of being the person who knows the *right* answer?

More often than not, we correct others not for their need to be corrected, but for our need to feel superior, valuable, or needed. It's the spirit of competition again.

A few clarifying questions:

- *Does this mistake actually affect anyone?*
- *Does this mistake change the main meaning of the message?*
- *Will pointing out this error do more harm than good?*
- *Would I want to be corrected on this, in this time and place?*
- *Is this actually a mistake at all, or just a difference?*

If the mistake is doing no harm or is really just you being pedantic, let it go. If pointing out a mistake doesn't add any value... then it's just a criticism.

Correcting people's pronunciation and grammar may veer into plain old snobbery or intolerance for genuine linguistic variation (not to mention, *you* could be the one who's wrong).

Tune into the deeper message being communicated and choose not to get hung up on the mechanics. No pedantry, just real understanding.

**A note on self-correction**

Getting sidetracked by trivial details can stall a conversation—even if you're the one correcting yourself. There is a conversational habit that has no name but is instantly recognizable. It goes like this. You are relating some story or anecdote, and you make a mistake or struggle to recall some detail or other.

So, you pause. You have a little conversation with yourself, "Now what was it? Have I got that right? Or maybe it was..."

A variation is that you stumble, stutter, or have trouble getting your mouth around a particular phrase. Rather than dwelling on it at length, getting flustered, or making a big show of correcting yourself, though, just say the correct thing and move swiftly on.

Otherwise, it's the equivalent of having a standup comedian stop to take a boring phone call right in the middle of his set. It's unnecessary, and it's *painful*.

The details don't matter! If you can't remember something, or if you've made a slight error, just move on—prioritize flow over accuracy.

**Abel Stevens said that politeness is the art of choosing among one's real thoughts.**

**People aren't perfect, and neither are conversations. Nevertheless, choose to focus on what's right, what's interesting, and what's enjoyable about the conversation. Let the rest go.**

## Chapter 12. Treat Every Comment Like a Personal Attack

OK, we know that we shouldn't be conversational takers, correct people unnecessarily, compete, compare, overshare, give unsolicited advice, or generally be domineering jerks.

But now, let's switch gears and consider things from the other side. **It's good to refrain from giving offense, but it's also good to refrain from taking it unnecessarily.**

Sensitivity and insecurity can tempt us into taking things personally when we really shouldn't. It may sound strange, but being overly ready to assume that you are being attacked is not all that different from being oblivious to how you may be attacking others.

Both stem from a tendency to center ourselves and relate everything that happens back to us.

- Maybe someone gives us feedback, and we feel embarrassed and personally targeted. "This is not fair."
- Maybe someone doesn't share our opinion as much as we'd like, and we get offended and think, "They don't respect me."

- Maybe someone corrects us and we feel a little misunderstood and hard done by. "They think I'm not good enough."

Even playful teasing can leave us feeling attacked.

This kind of defensiveness is pretty common, but unfortunately if you hold this frame, your focus shifts onto self-protection. And so long as you're focused on yourself, you're not present, and you're not connecting.

You may stop listening and shut down entirely.

How many mild disagreements, ruptures, and bad vibes are created not because someone genuinely intends to hurt us, but because of our decision to *perceive* things that way? Once things are framed in terms of victim/aggressor, even if only subtly, then the end of harmonious connection isn't far behind.

Humans are sociable creatures, and there's a reason we've evolved to take our fellow tribe members' opinions of us seriously. However, an underappreciated communication skill is learning to not absorb everything as a personal judgment or threat.

**We can stay grounded, present, and connected without turning every bit of friction into an attack on our worth.**

This is the other side of the winner/loser binary—but in just the same way as we don't need to fight to be on top, we don't need to assume that others are trying to put us down.

Take a look at some of the reasons why people make a habit of taking things personally:

- Negative self-talk about what events mean
- Perfectionism and unrealistic expectations
- Childhood trauma and poor self-esteem
- Anxiety, stress, and fatigue
- Finally, let's be honest, a habit of taking on the role of the victim

Notice a theme? None of these have anything to do with the other person, nor the real-life conversation that may be unfolding in the present moment. Taking things personally is not only the result of disconnection, but also the cause.

How do you break the cycle?

## **Respond to the Topic, Not the Tone**

When someone gives you feedback or disagrees with you, pause for a moment.

Understand that your emotional threat detection mechanisms may be triggered, and that you may be tempted to zoom in on the perceived emotional attack. You might be suddenly hyper-aware of their tone, their phrasing, the facial expression—*how* they said what they did.

The mind can play a little trick on us here: "I feel hurt; therefore, someone hurt me." That may not be true, though.

Zoom out again. Come out of your own emotion and see if you can identify *what* they were actually trying to say, rather than how they said it.

**In moments of potentially hurt feelings or misunderstandings, connect to the content, not the delivery.** Instead of focusing on how you feel, focus on what has literally been said.

If someone says, "Wow, I don't know if I can eat all this," when you prepare a meal, notice that little twinge that has you feeling criticized.

"Are they saying I've made too much? Implying they don't like the food? That I'm going overboard?"

But the truth is, all this angst comes from the interpretation, not the message itself. Look at it again: *I don't know if I can eat all this.* If we don't relate any part of this message back to ourselves, we can see it for what it is: They're simply expressing that they doubt their ability to eat that much.

Keep the conversation focused on clarity, not on the hurt feelings, or who to blame for them! Maintain a neutral, problem-solving mindset. Give people the benefit of the doubt and actively choose to be slow to upset.

## **Ask for Specifics Instead of Reading Between the Lines**

Taking things personally is often just the art of making assumptions and essentially hurting our own feelings. We assume there's a hidden jab somewhere and get to work trying to figure it out—and just like that we're disconnected again.

If something feels off to you, don't retreat into a private guessing game where you try to decipher and interpret their emotions to see whether you've been slighted or not.

**Instead, just ask.**

There's no need to jump to conclusions if you can deliberately uncover the facts.

- "Just so I'm understanding you here, are you saying you disagree with the plan itself, or just how I've explained it in the presentation?"
- "I might be hearing that differently than you mean it. Can you explain what you mean when you say...?"

- "Sorry, I'm not sure I've understood. Can you just walk me through that again?"

Even if someone *did* mean to cause a little offense, phrases like the above give them a get-out card and invite them to try again with more politeness. It's a trick that saves more relationships than you can imagine!

Clear up misunderstandings before they happen, rather than running with ambiguities and making them mean more than they need to. Hurt feelings are often nothing more than momentary misalignments. When you pause to clarify, one of a few things will happen: either you'll realize there's no offense to be taken, or you'll realize there is a criticism, but it's not quite as bad as you thought.

### **Use Curiosity Instead of Correction**

When we're feeling personally affronted, it's natural to want to push back in some way. We might argue, defend ourselves, "correct" them or reassert our position some way… perhaps by returning the jab.

Unsurprisingly, this tends not to help the conversation in any way. After all, if the other person takes the same approach, then they'll view your resistance as a thing to push back against, and before you know it, the conversation is over and the tug-of-war has begun.

Whether someone has been careless in their tone or not, hold yourself with dignity and simply ask them to expand on their view. Show a real interest in hearing what they have to say. It may prickle the ego a little to let them say *more* of what you're already finding uncomfortable to hear, but this feeling will pass quickly.

Someone may say, "This report is fine, but it's not really addressing the objectives, and the final section is just repetition."

You could respond with resistance:

- "Actually, every single objective has been clearly addressed in the first section. It's even in bold."
- "I've been doing the reports like that for years, and nobody has ever said anything about them until now."
- "I suppose you could do better?"

Or, you could take a breath and choose not to be reactive. Instead, you could say something like:

- "That's interesting. Can you talk me through exactly what makes you feel that way?"

If you can gently shift into curiosity and neutral problem-solving, you downregulate all the tension and fear that's making you want to kick off and declare war. Instead, show a sign that you're here to engage, not start a boxing match. Show that you're listening to understand, not to defend.

Make them feel heard, and they'll soften their message. The softer their message, the less attacked you'll feel. The less attacked you feel, the less defensive you'll be. Sometimes it's necessary to be the one to lay down your shield and take a step forward.

At the very least, it's a total power move, and helps you maintain your poise and dignity.

### **But What If It Really IS an Attack?**

Sometimes, you perceive a slight because there is one.

Even still, the frame we place around the actions and words of others makes all the difference.

- Just because someone is unhappy, it doesn't necessarily mean that you are to blame for it, or that it's now your responsibility to make them happy again.
- For the most part, people's opinions of you are actually about them, not you.

- Someone disagreeing with or disliking you is not a threat or an insult. It's just normal. There are a variety of perspectives on this planet. That person's perspective is valid; so is yours. There is no danger.
- Even if you do have unflattering flaws and have made mistakes, remind yourself that these things don't permanently define who you are. Remember that you have positive qualities, too. This is the heart of resilience.
- There is freedom, serenity, and clarity in simply refusing to consider your worth and value up for debate—whether the insults are real or imagined.

**Taking offense is as bad as giving offense because the effect is the same. Choose connection instead. Choose to put down your indignation and find your way back to the flow again.**

## Chapter 13. Cut People Off Mid-Sentence

Good conversations have rhythm. This rhythm is like a satisfying musical call-and-response, or like two dancers in perfect sync with one another.

Interrupting people—that's hitting a bad note or stomping on your partner's foot.

**Cutting someone off mid-thought is a subtle way to elevate your own flow and expression above theirs.** If you jump in, quickly finish their sentence for them or interject with something that takes the conversation in an entirely different direction, you're no longer being a team player, but breaking away to freestyle it.

The result? The other person feels dismissed, and like what they were saying was not important enough to hold your attention. Trouble brews quickly then; because they feel irritated and unseen, they may in turn retreat a little and quietly rehearse a rebuttal to knock *you* off the soap box.

In this way, interruptions can be like the million tiny paper cuts that eventually kill.

They're small, they don't feel significant in the moment, but they nevertheless chip away at trust and rapport. Conversational flow gets a little choppy. Before you know it, your conversation is really like two parallel monologues.

The important thing is that the damage gets done whether you intend it or not. Often the reasons for cutting people off are totally benign:

- You're excited
- You're distracted
- You're in a hurry
- You're "helping"

Yet carelessness in conversation can do as much damage as malice.

Accidental interruptions do happen, but they're simple to cut down:

- Stay present.
- Relax—it's not a race or competition.
- Be aware of the overall tone and pace of the conversation. Match it, rather than trying to hurry and get ahead of it.
- Listen. Be less preoccupied with sharing what you know and more interested in catching everything *they're* sharing.

**When It's OK to Interrupt**

What about those people who drone on and on and would simply never stop unless you forcefully butted your way in again? Are we doomed to sit quietly and never chip in when someone else is talking? Thankfully, no!

**Certain interruptions serve a noble function**—they act as helpful guardrails for speakers who may have lost their way a little, or polite cues to alert someone that it's time to hand over the talking stick, so to speak. If time is of the essence, an interruption may be unavoidable.

The truth is that no matter how good at communication *we* get, we will still regularly encounter others who have, shall we say, not been burdened with an overabundance of training in this area.

There is an art to interrupting kindly, respectfully, and productively. We don't have to be at the mercy of conversational narcissists. Below are some things to consider when interrupting *tactfully*.

## Before the Chat Gets Long-Winded: Ask for Permission to Jump In

Theoretically, kindness and active listening are unlimited. What *isn't* unlimited? Time.

Interrupting properly becomes a matter of etiquette. Think of it not as being rude, but as carefully pruning away all those tangents that would otherwise derail a good chat and get it lost in the weeds.

- Maybe you're delivering a speech or presentation, and somebody has a "question" that is really just an attempt to seize the floor and air their own opinions. At length.
- Maybe you're politely checking in on an elderly neighbor on your way to work, but in no time he's offloading a dreary backstory and anecdote you never wanted to know about in the first place.
- Or maybe you're on a date with someone who seems to have gotten caught in a loop, reiterating ground already well-covered, when you'd rather just have fun.

Interrupting early on in a conversation that looks like it's going this way is a *teeny tiny* inconvenience that will spare you a lot of awkwardness later on. Get ahead of someone before the conversation gets lost in circles.

Over-explainers and people who don't know when to stop elaborating need someone to set a boundary, and tag, you're it.

Say:

- "Mind if I jump in quickly? I'm just aware that we only have an hour, and I want to make sure we're leaving ourselves enough time to cover everything."

- "Sorry to interrupt. That's a really good point, but I wonder if we might like to save that for later, when we have more time? For now, I was wondering what you thought about [actual agenda]."
- "Forgive me for butting in, but I wanted to say I'm pleased we're on the same page on this. Unless there's still something else we're not in agreement on, shall we call it a day for now?"

**Show that your wish to cut them short is actually in the interests of the bigger picture.** Frame your interruption in terms of efficiency and respect for the broader aims, rather than on rushing, dismissing, or devaluing their contribution.

It's a delicate balance sometimes, but you can't go wrong if you interrupt firmly while simultaneously laying on the praise.

"Excuse me Lydia, sorry to interrupt, but I wanted to say that that's a really good observation you've made there. In fact, it leads us neatly to why I've asked to speak to everyone today..."

**Validate, acknowledge, and be polite... but firmly steer things back on course again.**

## **If They Don't Stop Talking: Use a Visual Cue to Signal You'd Like to Speak**

They are medical marvels. Those people who can talk and talk and talk and never need to take a breath.

There's no natural pause or gap.

Nowhere to squeeze the word in edgeways, as they say.

If you hope to make a dent in that wall of words, you're forced to cut them off mid-speech.

Luckily for us, verbal communication is not the only channel we have open to us. If you can't find a foothold verbally, seek one *non*verbally:

- Raise your hand a little (yes, like you did in school!)
- Part your lips as though you're preparing to speak
- Shift forward or lean in
- Clear your throat or draw an obvious breath

If someone is caught in the reveries of their own monologue, they may simply be too distracted holding court to notice their audience, so don't be afraid to make your gesture a tiny bit more obvious than seems necessary.

Send a polite but assertive nonverbal cue—it's a way to interrupt without interrupting. If this is ignored, you can resort to a more obvious verbal interruption or even make use of humor or some distraction in the immediate environment to pump the brakes.

"OK, woah, I have to stop you there. I'm going to need a few minutes to process all that... oh by the way, the waiter's over there. Do you want me to order you another latte?"

If you've built enough rapport and flow until that point, and you use plenty of open and friendly body language, this kind of interruption should get the message across without causing offense.

## **When They're Off-Track: Acknowledge, Then Gently Redirect the Conversation**

Sometimes it's not that people are speaking too much or not taking turns, it's that they're rambling or veering way, way of topic. Not everyone goes into every conversation with a clear and pre-prepared agenda. Some people have not clearly thought through what they hope to get from the conversation—indeed, the conversation itself is how they think through things.

When you find yourself trapped in a meandering dialogue with a person in this frame of mind, first things first: relax. Let yourself off the hook. You do *not* need to sacrifice your time and energy on the altar of politeness. You do *not* need to hand the conversation over to them to get mangled out of shape.

People overexplain for a variety of reasons.

- They're anxious.
- They're tired.
- They're distracted.
- Perhaps they simply have different preferences or expectations of the conversation.

Whatever it is, be firm and polite as you redirect, while acknowledging where the need may be coming from. You don't need to apologize—after all, you're a part of the conversation too. But you will only stress yourself out trying to accommodate their rambling. Try:

- "That makes a lot of sense. Can I pause you real quick? I think we're pretty much in agreement on that. Tell me about [insert topic that's more on track]."
- "I totally get that. Let me jump in for a second, though. I think I recall we had

planned to talk about [agenda] today, right?"
- "Oh interesting! Sorry to cut you off, but I think we have covered that? I know it's hard to keep track."

Validate what's been said, then move the conversation forward. Make things feel collaborative, not dismissive.

**Listening to others is a form of respect. You can be patient, kind, and respectful... and still be focused and on-track. It's never either-or.**

## Chapter 14. Drizzle Everything with Sarcasm

Oscar Wilde once said that "Sarcasm is the lowest form of wit, but the highest form of intelligence."

Here's what he might have meant:

- Being able to perceive ambiguity in statements and read multiple interpretations in a phrase—that's smart.
- Using confusion as humor—that's *not* smart.

Sarcasm is defined as the "use of irony to mock or convey contempt." Sarcasm is caustic, destructive, and designed to cut—but it's also weaselly and indirect, often hiding behind ambivalence. Sarcasm may or may not be ironic, and it may or may not be funny.

The one thing it always is? Kinda mean.

**Sarcasm may make people laugh, but it doesn't build trust.**

Satire and irony can seem clever, but the humor often lies in confusing people—they recognize that something is afoot, but they can't quite tell if they've been insulted or not. Sarcastic jokes and jabs may seem obvious to you, but their entire mechanism rests on ambiguity, which taxes other people's goodwill and politeness.

If people don't understand or share your humor, if they don't know you well, or if they're simply not in the mood, then sarcasm can come across as selfish and slightly juvenile. Sarcasm may not carry well across different cultures or age groups, so your dazzling wit may land as criticism or simply leave the listener scratching their head.

Funny, *maybe*. But that's a slim payoff when weighed up against the potential risks. When sarcasm flops, it's never neutral; the fallout is an instant drop in clarity, politeness, and connection.

**Set aside your own need to be perceived as sharp and witty, and prioritize openness, respect, and clarity instead.**

It's rude to put people off balance. While you may sincerely want to bring some playfulness and zing to a conversation, understand that those who make a habit out of sarcasm risk being perceived as haughty and self-absorbed. If you're *not* haughty and self-absorbed, read on for ways to bring in some fun and sass without accidentally causing hurt.

## **Don't Assume They'll Catch Your Tone**

Jokes, kidding around, and good-natured ribbing are great ways to bring energy and levity to a conversation. But you have to be smart about it.

Sarcasm won't work if the other person doesn't pick up on context clues, nonverbal communication, timing, or tone.

A study has found that men and women perceive sarcasm slightly differently, and that different age groups have different ways of resolving ambiguity. Brits and Americans unsurprisingly have different opinions on what counts as rude, and people's ability to catch sarcasm varies depending on context, the format of the message (for example text, email, or face to face), or just how they're feeling that day (Makarla et. al., 2024).

That's a lot of caveats, a lot of different ways for even the most finely crafted sarcasm to fall flat.

You can bring in all the benefits of sarcasm—playfulness, lightness, fun, a little chemistry—*without* bringing in the risks of sarcasm. How?

- Make jokes, but ones that are *unmistakably* jokes. Forgeo some cleverness if it means being more obvious.

- If you must poke fun at something, let it be yourself or the situation, never the other person.
- Save the spicier banter for people you know well. A good rule of thumb for everyone else is to match and reflect their tone.

**If you're in doubt, don't.** Direct communication may not win you any amateur comedian points, but neither will it leave people feeling hurt or bewildered. It's almost always better to be polite, warm, and friendly, rather than attempting humor... and relying on someone else's emotional decoding to make it work.

## Swap Sarcasm for Teasing That Feels Mutual

It usually feels better to dish out sarcasm than to receive it. This form of humor carries more than the faintest whiff of superiority to it, which alone can have others feeling that you're laughing at their expense. Sarcasm isn't humor, and it isn't a sign of intelligence. It's low-key hostility.

A gentler alternative: teasing.

Teasing is sarcasm's nicer younger sibling who kids around without losing a sense of mutual affection.

According to Makarla and her colleagues, teasing is more polite. But what's the difference?

**Sarcasm**:

- Often delivered in a lower, slower voice, and with a "deadpan" expression
- You're laughing *at* them
- They're outside of the joke
- Creates confusion and subtly lowers the other person

**Teasing**:

- Often delivered with a warm smile
- You're laughing *with* them
- They're in on the joke with you
- Clear and direct, and subtly elevates the other person

Compare:

- **Sarcasm**: "Wow, congrats. You totally nailed it." (Said with flat expression and bored tone of voice).
- **Teasing**: "You silly goose, you're such a mess! But I love you anyway." (Said with a big grin and delivered with a hug).
- **Sarcasm**: "Please, take your time, it's not like I had plans to do anything today."

- **Teasing**: "Come on let's go already! You know I'm not cool enough to be fashionably late to things!"

There simply is no point in triggering other people's defensiveness. The very best thing that can happen is that they laugh it off or come back with an even wittier retort. Though a duo comedy act may be funny for a while, you're missing out on the good stuff—real connection.

## **Match Your Style to the Setting—and the Person**

Before you go in with a snide remark, make a joke, or get sassy, ask yourself:

- "Do I know this person well enough that this joke will come across as playful?"
- "Is this the right time?"
- "Is this the right place?"
- "What's more important now—cleverness or kindness?"
- "What kind of conversation is this—trivial, sensitive, professional, romantic, casual?"
- "Being honest, am I trying to contribute to the flow and connection, or am I just trying to make myself look intelligent or superior?"

Clumsy remarks can tank even solid friendships, so it's best not to make assumptions. If you crack a joke and it doesn't land, whatever you do, *don't double down*. Quickly laugh it off, clarify your tone and move on.

If someone hasn't responded like you'd hoped, one of the worst things you can do is to make *them* feel bad about it. People who insist that something is funny when someone else doesn't get it isn't a comedian… they're a bully.

**Mark Twain said that humor is the good-natured side of truth. Be playful, be silly, be lighthearted, and don't take things seriously—but do it in a good-natured way.**

## Chapter 15. Be a Judge Judy

Humans like putting things into categories.

We sort things: This vs. that; like me vs. not like me; important vs. not important.

But there's one categorization that can get us into trouble when it comes to communicating effectively: the distinctions we make between *good* and *bad*.

Look, being able to discern between right and wrong is a valuable instinct. Without forming an opinion or judgment about something's value, we could never identify what food is good to eat, which people might be dangerous, and what behavior might not help us reach our goal.

The trouble of course is that our tendency to judge can also get in the way of us receiving new information, being open to other perspectives, and possibly being corrected.

- **Discernment**: Forming a reasonable opinion based on objective information. That's a useful tool.
- **Judgment**: Forming preconceived opinions without basis in real evidence. That's liable to get in the way of real connection.

Even if we don't like to think of ourselves as judgmental people, we may be unintentionally using *judgmental language* that puts distance between us and others. Intention matters, but people cannot read into our minds and hearts. All they can respond to is the verbal and nonverbal communication with which we're expressing ourselves.

### **Letting Go of the Need to Evaluate**

**When we label something as good or bad, right or wrong, we are evaluating it.**

Let's skip right over the part where we debate whether our appraisal is correct or not.

It may be. It may not be.

What's important here is what this tendency does to a conversation, and the subtle shift in tone that occurs once we start using language of evaluation.

When we make the call to announce what we think something is worth (that is, we make a value judgment), then we have changed the feeling of the interaction. We are not just experiencing something, but rating, ranking, and assessing it.

Just like that, there are stakes. Just like that it's now possible to be found wanting. Little nuances of competition and threat can enter where before there may have been simple openness and presence.

Judgment can creep in ever so slightly. But while you may not have noticed it, the other person almost certainly did. People are naturally sensitive to perceived criticism or rejection, so they might pick up on all those unspoken assumptions that you have not fully acknowledged in yourself.

How do you respond when you feel judged?

If you're like most people, you:

- Retreat
- Defend
- Attack
- ...or a mix of all three

Judgements lead to damaged rapport. That juicy conversational flow dries up. Importantly, judgment doesn't even have to be blatant to have this effect.

For those of us who have a hard time dropping the judgment habit, it can seem genuinely impossible to go about life *without* appraising the value of people, things, and ideas. But the trick is to realize that we can observe, experience, listen, and be open to whatever is unfolding in the present moment... without rushing in to decide what we think about it.

**In other words, perception and evaluation are two different things.**

It's the difference between seeing something and saying, "That's bad," and seeing it and asking, "What is that?"

**Judgement shuts things down. Curiosity, reflection, and presence opens them up again.**

At the very least, wean yourself off of the habit by thinking, "I can be judgy all I want... later. For now, I'm just noticing."

Let's take a closer look at how this attitude plays out in everyday conversations.

### Drop the Labels—Say What You Saw, Not What You Think It Means

- "You're being so sensitive."
- "That was weird."
- "He's always been a commitment-phobe."

It might not look like it, but these statements are dripping with judgment. They are not mere observations, even though they may pretend to be. Rather, they contain evaluations and assign meaning and value.

Labels are one of the sneakiest ways we can be tempted to dip into judgment. Commitment-phobe. Sensitive. During active listening, putting a label on an emotion can certainly be a kind and constructive thing to do for someone ("You sound upset" or "Do you think it's nervousness?") but labels can quickly become judgmental when we use them to *add in* our own estimations, rather than just making neutral observations.

**Instead, stick to the facts**. Remember that perception and evaluation are two different things.

- Perception: "This is a nettle bush."
- Judgement: "This is a nasty weed that shouldn't be here, and I don't like it."

To take the judgment out of your own language, keep focused on what you observe—not what you think those observations *mean*. Slow down and recognize the two steps here, and deliberately choose to delay that second step, where you weigh in with your own interpretations.

**Descriptive language** is clean, direct, and neutral. We convey the facts without attaching meaning and value, without interpretation, and without jumping to conclusions. We're clear and unambiguous.

- Judgmental: "You're being so sensitive."

- Descriptive: "I noticed you stopped talking after that feedback in the meeting. You OK?"
- Judgmental: "That was weird."
- Descriptive: "I haven't heard that kind of music before. I didn't expect that!"
- Judgmental: "He's always been a commitment-phobe."
- Descriptive: "He's had a few relationships. They tend not to last longer than a few months."

Staying in descriptive mode not only spares you from accidentally assigning blame or causing offense, it will also dampen the tendency to complain or gossip. Descriptive language seldom invites people's defensiveness—and that's a win for you.

Try not to be vague or make sweeping generalizations. Drop the need to categorize into right or wrong, or to assign an emotive label. See if you can remove "right" and "wrong" from your vocabulary entirely, and instead of deciding whether it's right or wrong, just notice what it *is*.

When we are non-judgmental, we allow people to trust us and open up further.

**A note on "positive judgments"**

Praise has its place, and validation can go a long way, but be aware that this isn't neutral, descriptive language.

Though far less common a phenomenon, it is possible to create conversational ruptures with *positive* judgments. After all, they're still evaluations. With them we still establish ourselves as judge and jury, instead of just remaining open and present without needing to weigh things up.

- "You're being very brave." (But what if I just want you to acknowledge how afraid I feel?)
- "You're a giver, you always have been." (But I need to talk about the possibility of changing.)
- "You're doing the best you can." (Maybe I'm not, and I don't want the sweet talk!)

Judgment gets in the way because it prematurely shuts down exploration and understanding in favor of foregone conclusions—whether those conclusions are flattering or not.

Lively, dynamic conversation acknowledges people where they are, as they are, right now. It does not saddle them with labels, even if those labels are complimentary.

- Instead of, "Don't worry, you've got this!" ask, "How do you feel?"
- Instead of, "Your performance was amazing!" ask, "I enjoyed that. Are you pleased with your performance?"

## **Ask Curiously, Not Critically**

We can bring in judgment via the questions we ask. A judgy question is more of an accusation than a sincere request to learn more:

- "Why would you even do that?"
- "Did you really think this was a good idea?"
- "Why aren't you getting this?"

Let's reframe to bring in some genuine interest, care, and empathy:

- "What made you decide on that path?"
- "Could you talk me through your thought process here?"
- "What is causing the most confusion for you right now?"

When you ask a question with real curiosity, you invite your conversation partner to open up and tell a story.

When you ask a question with judgment, you push them to defend themselves or retreat.

Making a judgment is a last-step kind of move. We gather information, then we arrive at our conclusion. But if we *start* with a judgment, we've already come to a conclusion without having gathered any information. And if we already know all there is to know about a situation, then there's no point in talking further, right?

Advice, opinions, and pronouncements tend to end a conversation, rather than open it up to a real resolution. If you're in the middle of a conflict or disagreement, focus on communicating a desire to understand. Instead of offering advice, opinions, or assessments, offer honest observations and ask for more information.

Don't load up your questions with hidden assumptions and biases. Instead, use them to genuinely seek out understanding. Set your own opinion and perspective aside and ask,

- "What is this person's story?"
- "How are they seeing things? What things are they seeing?"
- "What's going on in their world right now?"

Pay attention to what is unfolding in the moment, without trying to interpret what it means, especially not what it means to you personally. If you're stumped, you can't go wrong with some general expressions of active listening and empathy:

- "That makes sense."
- "I hear what you're saying."
- "Tell me more."

The truth is that it can be a huge relief to let go of the judgment habit. It's a real "Aha!" moment to realize that our appraisal isn't necessary for a conversation to proceed.

Even if we do have an opinion, that doesn't mean we have to stop listening or connecting. We can delay forming an opinion. We can even (gasp!) choose not to have an opinion at all.

## **Reflect Back, Don't Weigh In**

Imagine you're telling your mother about your recent back pain problems. You're grumpy, you're sore, and you're tired of getting the runaround from the doctors. Now take a look at the following responses she might give, and see what each one makes you feel:

a) "You should see a chiropractor."
b) "Your mattress is too soft, that's why."
c) "A little back ache is just part of getting older, you'll get used to it."
d) "Are you sure it's back pain? Maybe you're just slouching too much."

The reason none of these responses feel especially satisfying is that they don't address the emotional reason you're complaining about your back pain in the first place. You want sympathy, not a lecture!

**When people judge and weigh in, it's a little like giving unsolicited advice—while completely ignoring the unspoken request for listening, support, and validation.**

Many of us are a little too used to responding with our own advice, opinions, or perceptions. We assume we are being prompted to make a suggestion, cast a verdict, or decide what we personally think.

Sometimes, without knowing it, we put ourselves in the position of validating the speaker's own responses. With our judgmental ears on, we mistakenly think it's our job to verify or confirm what's being said, rather than just to receive it.

- "Don't be silly, you have nothing to be scared of."
- "You should be grateful."
- "Did he really say that? Maybe you misunderstood."

But when people open up to us, sometimes the best thing we can do for them is just to witness, hold, and reflect what we've heard—

no extra spin. Echo back the emotion you're picking up, without adding anything.

Do this by paraphrasing emotions, but don't put words into their mouths, like this:

- They say, "I'm just feeling so *scared*."
- You say, "I hear you. It does sound like quite a *frightening* time."

Be present as a listener and witness, without appointing yourself authority over their life. It's not your job to decide how their experience weighs up, how it compares to yours, or how reasonable and justified their rection is.

Your job is to step momentarily outside of your world and step into theirs. This is no big loss. Your world will be right there where you left it!

**Our conversation partners don't need us to *evaluate* them. They need us to *acknowledge* them. Don't show up with your mind already made up about how things are; instead, open up to the possibility of finding out how things actually are.**

## Chapter 16. Tell Stories That Are Convoluted and/or Tedious

There are few sincerely boring people in the world. Everyone has a story to tell.

However, the *way* they tell that story makes a big, big difference.

Boring stories kill conversations. It's not because the people sharing them are boring, nor that the events in question are boring. Rather, the story's format is where the dullness comes from.

- No structure.
- No tension.
- No direction.

**Boring stories are boring because they're meandering and pointless.** They're a string of loosely connected data points offered one after the other, and the payoff, if there is one, comes way too late.

Boring stories are shapeless. They're fluffy and they don't give listeners enough reason to keep on listening. The result is that people pay attention for as long as politeness demands, but fatigue eventually wins and ultimately, they just tune out.

When your story wanders, so too will the attention of your audience.

We all know what a great story feels like, but how exactly do you create one from scratch?

The good news is that you don't have to be a naturally charming or entertaining personality, and your story doesn't need to be outrageously unusual or amusing. **Get the *structure* right, and you're halfway there.**

Randy Olson first outlined what he calls his ABT structure in *Houston, We Have a Narrative* (University of Chicago Press, 2015). Good storytelling is not magic, he explains, but an art that you can learn to master. Get the recipe right and you too can cook up a narrative that people will really relish.

Olson started life as a scientist, but ended up reskilling as a filmmaker, where he realized that scientists could learn a lot from Hollywood. Presenting a dry collection of scientific facts will never be enough, he said; we need *narrative*. It's what the human mind is built for, it's what it wants, and it's how it understands the world.

In fact, this broad structure is so built into the way human beings process information that you could use the ABT approach for all sorts of things: telling compelling anecdotes, shaping a scientific report, or simply making a persuasive argument.

The formula is easy:

Beginning, middle, and end.

**ABT – AND, BUT, and THEREFORE.**

- AND: First set the scene with two essential facts that lay out a status quo or current problem.
- BUT: Then introduce the twist, tension, or conflict. Highlight a snag, a contradiction, or a sudden change to the status quo just identified.
- THEREFORE: Finally, deliver the resulting consequence or realization. Resolve the tension you've just created with a solution or outcome that brings the story to a close.

Even if your listeners are unaware of this framework, they will respond emotionally to the sense of psychological completeness it offers—even if your "story" is just 15 seconds long.

Following this structure provides a few vital advantages:

- It forces you to get clear on the main message you're trying to convey—which means you'll waffle less.

- Since each segment leads neatly onto the next, you won't get bogged down with irrelevant details or bore people.
- You'll be delivering a *story*—not just a string of facts. And that means your listeners are not just engaging their brains, but their emotions, too.
- You know when you're done. There's a punchline and a clear payoff, making it easy to see exactly where you stop and hand over the reins to someone else.

ABT stories feel more entertaining, more complete, and more logical because of their structure. It's an intuitively satisfying shape that is behind all the most effective speeches, jokes, and anecdotes.

It only takes three easy steps:

1. Set the stage.
2. Introduce an element of tension.
3. Resolve that tension and give the audience a kind of "Aha!" moment.

Your listeners will be unconsciously *expecting* this format. As a storyteller, you enter into a kind of unspoken agreement with your listener: in return for them paying you their attention, you're expected to lead them skillfully down a path, at the end of which is something new, interesting, or fun.

If you *don't* lead them on this journey, you're basically disrespecting this unspoken contract. If your listeners start to suspect that there's nothing at the end of the path you're leading them down, it's understandable that they'll quietly withdraw the attention they initially invested.

Let's take a closer look at how to use the ABT structure to craft stories that will reward your listener's attention, build warmth and rapport, and create good conversational energy.

### **Don't Overload the "AND"**

Most stories are boring because, frankly, they're not stories at all. People open their mouths, stuff comes out, and they only close them again when they're interrupted or need to come up for air.

That may be a slight exaggeration, but it's true to say that most stories need far less background than we think they do. We don't need to lay out the full family lineage of every character in the story, nor do we need to establish the precise location, date, time, or weather at the time of the anecdote.

Two little snippets are usually more than enough. For example:

> "We were at the science museum once *and* we had just made our way to their moon landing exhibit."

Two facts: We were at the science museum, and we were checking out the moon landing exhibit. There's the AND.

Just like that, the scene is set perfectly. No need to explain at length how much you paid to get in, the other exhibits they had on, or what you had for breakfast that morning. If you give too much contextual information, your poor audience will be frantically listening for a point. "Is he about to tell me a story about breakfast? Oh no, wait, this is about money. Or is it dinosaurs?"

If you pad your story with too many details, you confuse your listener's narrative impulse and wear out their patience. They may eventually just tune out, thinking, "It's fine, I'll wake up again when he gets to the point."

## **Make the "BUT" Juicy and Relatable**

In real life, things just happen, one thing after another.

**Stories are not structured like real life; we need to *add* the framework.**

In a story, things are the way they are, then they get worse, then perhaps they get even worse, but then they get better. That is the shape of a story.

The second part of the ABT frame is where we throw in the curveball, the interruption, or the unexpected turn:

- *Everything was fine until one day, a stranger came to town.*
- *They finished setting up 500 seats outdoors when they all noticed the dark clouds on the horizon...*
- *She took an enormous bite, swallowed it, and then saw the label: Warning, for animal consumption only.*

You've set the scene, and now you're introducing the heart of your story. This shift alone keeps the story moving forward and will have people paying close attention.

The tension and delight come from presenting the BUT and then letting it linger there for a moment. This draws the listener in. It's human nature—we want to see what happens next.

Notice, of course, that you don't have to technically use the word "but." What is important is that you clearly signal the narrative change. Done well, these signals will pique your listener's curiosity.

## **Stick the Landing with a Clean "THEREFORE"**

The last step is for wrapping things up. What happened next?

A neat and clean resolution is one that is concise—*don't overexplain.* Be quick, be clear, be done. Don't give your story a flabby tail by continuing to elaborate long after the punchline has been delivered. **End where the energy ends.**

> "Long story short, we spent the night in the ER. Not quite the first date we expected!"

In the moment, it may feel extremely tempting to elaborate, but the best endings are short and sweet, and put a clear, defined conclusion to things. Think of it as a little "Ta da!" or bow at the end of a performance—it's a tiny cue to signal to your listener that it's their turn to react and switch the focus to another speaker.

Here's a quick story that does *not* follow the ABT format:

> "My friend Lucy had something like that happen to her. This was when she was still in the student dorms, actually, so not the house she's in now... have you met Lucy? No? Oh well anyway she actually ended up with three cats one

day instead of one. So, she had gone to the cat shelter and they told her they didn't have any black and white cats, because that was the kind she was after, right? She wanted a black and white male, a little older because she didn't want to housetrain a kitten and everything. And she has kids. She didn't have kids back then, now that I think of it, but she didn't want the responsibility of a kitten so she was looking for an older cat. A male. But they didn't have any. This was the St. Benedict's cat rescue, you know the one next to the pharmacy? I think your auntie volunteered there once..."

Yawn!

It's not at all clear what the *point* of this story is. Lucy is the main character, but is this a story about her housing situation? About cats…?

It appears that the punchline might be "she ended up with two cats instead of one" but then why all the additional details?

The order of events is kind of hard to follow, and it's not clear how each data point is related to the others. What role do Lucy's kids play in this story? Does Lucy start the story with two cats, or does she end with two? And what has your aunt got to do with anything?!

It's confusing. And it's boring AF.

Here's the same anecdote told with the ABT structure:

"My friend Lucy had always wanted a black and white cat but never found the right one. Finally, after years, she adopts a black and white cat from the shelter, and they tell her to come and pick him up the following day, right? *That night*, two stray cats—both black and white—show up on her doorstep and instantly make themselves at home. And just like that, she went from no black and white cats to *three*!"

Without structure, stories feel flabby and endless. With ABT, however, even the most insignificant little stories and anecdotes become charming and memorable.

**A few more hints and tips:**

- The narrative payoff is usually emotional, not informational. Be expressive and lean into the transformation of feelings: confusion to understanding, boredom to surprise, hope to satisfaction, etc.
- Play with anticipation but be quick. People's attention spans are shorter than you think, but they *are* willing to focus if the promise of narrative payoff

is big enough. Pose an intriguing question, be a little mysterious, pause dramatically... and then deliver the goods.
- Remember that humor doesn't have to be super clever or complex. A neat little tale delivered in a good-natured way is a safer bet than making deliberate attempts to be funny.

**Ira Glass said that great stories happen to those who can tell them. The best stories all follow a predictable and emotionally satisfying three-step structure.**

**People hate rambling, but they *love* stories. Tell them one.**

## Chapter 17. Treat Silence Like a Disease

For many of us, the unspoken rule is that silence = danger.

We treat silence as a terrifying sign that we have left the realm of comfortable conversation and are rapidly approaching Awkward Territory. Without knowing it, we may fear silence because we interpret it as judgment or criticism—as though the other person has found us boring.

The solution? Quickly say something—anything—to fill that gap and get things moving again.

In fact, research from the University of Groningen puts a number on it: four measly seconds of silence. That's all it takes to put people on edge in conversation—at least in what they call Anglophone countries (Koudenburg et. al., 2010).

In some cultures, silence is treated like a sign of conversational malfunction. We think that connection means talking, and so if nobody is talking, then something is wrong with the connection. Without realizing it, we may carry all sorts of assumptions about conversation: that extroverted, loud, and lively are always preferable to quiet, slow, and relaxed.

Those of us who struggle with social anxiety and the "don't know what to say" disease may fear silence as the ultimate failure. Cue the rush to fill that silence... which may actually create the awkwardness it was designed to alleviate.

**But what if silence isn't a bug, but a feature?**

In other countries, the attitude towards silence is different. The Japanese, for example, have been found to comfortably tolerate more than 8 seconds of silence (Yamada, 2015). Silence here means thoughtfulness and respect. It signals a pause for reflection, and, when used confidently, demonstrates power and impact.

The instinct to rush to fill silence means:

- We may say something ill-considered
- We come across as anxious and uncomfortable
- We may dilute our message or trivialize what we're saying
- We may offer premature conclusions that actually cut off meaningful connection, just as it was deepening

We do all of this to fix the "problem" of silence... but what if it wasn't a problem in the first place? How many times, after all, have you thought, "damn, this silence is embarrassing" and then promptly went on to fill that silence with something that was also embarrassing?

*Let's try to shift perspective a little.*

- Conversations flow.
- The rhythm, pace, and energy of a conversation changes, and that's normal.
- A silence or lull simply signifies a shift in rhythm.
- There's nothing to fix, because nothing's broken.

**Being comfortable with silence isn't about deliberately saying less. It's about being okay with not rushing to say more**. Silence happens. Getting good at being silent means learning to feel calm, present, and connected in that silence when it happens.

## Practice Silence Until It Feels Familiar

If silence has always felt weird to you, experiment with introducing little moments of quietness into your everyday routine. If you're used to having the radio on in the background, for example, practice turning it off sometimes, and just being present with whatever task you're doing. Leave your earbuds at home when you go for a walk.

The world is noisy and information-dense. The 24-hour news cycle, social media, TV... Try to notice the impulse to reach for these distractions, and instead challenge yourself to see what it's like to just let that impulse go, unheeded.

Silence can be really, really wonderful. Pause. Let your mind *settle*.

Notice what it does in the absence of constant stimuli.

Notice how quietness can bring a certain ease, flow, and comfort to things.

Notice what it feels like to be more deliberate, less reactive.

**Remember: Silence is *not* emptiness.**

**Silence is not just the absence of speech, but a conversational tool.**

The more familiar you are with stillness in day-to-day life, the less awkward it will feel when it crops up in a conversation.

### In Conversations, Wait TWO Seconds Before You Speak

Two or three seconds may not seem like much, but in the context of a conversation it can feel so much longer than it is.

**If there's a pause, notice it, but don't panic. Count to three in your head before speaking.** Silence can be an anxiety trigger, but it doesn't have to be. Train yourself to wait, even just a little.

This brings more space into your dialogue and lets things breathe a little.

Not rushing to fill that space has many happy side-effects:

- You relax. It's more about presence, and less about performance.
- You come across as more confident, more in control, and more poised.
- You give the other person's message time and space to unfold—they feel heard.
- You create a conversation that is more meaningful. Instead of anxious flitting from one topic to the next, you pace it. You breathe. You enjoy yourself.

Pauses often come after a message has been delivered. If you embrace that pause, you demonstrate that you've listened and are actually processing the message, rather than just blurting out a kneejerk response.

Give it a second. Skip a beat. You may just discover that they then add to the message and go a little further. That pause is what allows the real stuff to come out. Without pauses, you just kick the conversation along from one superficial topic to the next.

Silent pauses, on the other hand, allow things to sink in.

They invite depth.

### **Let Others Break the Silence First**

When things go quiet, we can sometimes think, "Oh no! Do something!" as though you alone were responsible for keeping the conversational engines going. But are you?

**Show a little faith in the other person and their ability to contribute.** You may be surprised by what people come up with when you just relax and stop trying to forcefully control the flow.

Nervous chatter can displace something meatier and more meaningful. It can also, over time, create the feeling that you alone are responsible for carrying the conversation—which we know is hard work! Instead, *share* the conversation, and it won't feel like work at all.

For example, let's say you're talking to a potential connection for work. They quote you a price that's higher than what your anticipated budget can handle. You say, "I'm sorry, but I'm just not sure I can afford all that."

Silence follows.

Here, you could jump in with more elaboration and give further details. But, if you just wait, then something else has the chance to happen.

They eventually say, "Honestly, I think we did overquote this time. We're OK with coming down on the price."

This is a revelation that might not have come had you filled the space up with anxious chatter.

**Conversations are co-creations**—give the other person enough room to contribute. Don't spoon feed, don't ramble, don't rush.

## Use Silence to Show You're Listening, Not Stuck

The temptation to rush in with a reaction or solution may be strong.

But if someone says something significant, realize that you can demonstrate respect and understanding without saying a word. You can be present and signal your concern and care in a totally nonverbal way.

The truth is that most people don't *want* a fast, down-pat response. It's far more impactful to just stay with them. It's more effective (and easier for you!) to show that you're someone people can talk to.

**Silence is a way to communicate presence. It says, "I'm here," in a way that the literal words never can!**

When you're silent, you're not passing judgment or making interpretations. You're just there. You're offering a steady stream of calm, unrushed attention. No agenda, no strain to come up with a quick response. There's beauty and simplicity in that.

**Silence is not awkward unless you make it so. Stillness is not the absence of communication; it's the wellspring.**

## Chapter 18. Apologize Like a Corporate Email

"Well, I'm sorry you feel that way."

Nothing makes someone less likely to forgive and forget than the above "apology."

Most of the conversational bad habits we've explored so far are misguided and will make connection and rapport harder to build. But crappy apologies? They don't just inhibit connection—they actively destroy it.

As human beings we all slip up now and again, and that means that we need to know how to handle things when we do. It matters that you apologize, but *how* you apologize is even more important.

A study published in *Negotiation and Conflict Management Research* (Lewicki, 2016) explains how there are six key features to an effective apology. If an apology contains all six, it has the greatest chance of mending a broken connection—or even making it stronger than before.

- Good apologies rebuild trust after breaches.
- Bad ones are registered as additional breaches.

**What should a good apology look like?**

First, let's think about what an apology is actually *for*.

When people feel wronged, it creates a kind of debt in the relationship. They want someone to be accountable, they want real empathy, and they want the wrongdoer to make genuine efforts to make things right again. Without any of these things in place, an apology will flop, no matter how polite and timely it is.

That's why most therapists and relationship experts agree: **An insincere apology is usually worse than no apology.**

Ineffective apologies are those where we are saying something just to be polite, or unconsciously shifting blame off of ourselves. It's not flattering to admit, but sometimes we apologize merely to minimize the impact of what we've done and take away the other person's grounds for grievance. "I said sorry, didn't I?"

But the real function of an apology is not damage control, technical box-ticking, or ego maintenance—it's restoration and healing. And that's an *emotional* function.

It's paying that emotional debt so that the connection can be restored.

If some breach has occurred, efforts need to be made to repair it. Unless an apology adequately meets this emotional need, it will fail—or risk causing even more offense.

Done wrong, an apology can hurt feelings, shatter trust, and trigger more arguments. But done right, it's a chance to repair connections or even strengthen connections. Here are the six elements to include if you want to do it properly.

## **<u>Say What You Regret, and Mean It</u>**

**Express genuine regret.**

The other person needs to see—and believe—your remorse.

It's not enough to simply acknowledge that *they've* been hurt or inconvenienced by our actions; we have to demonstrate that we ourselves are also unhappy about what has occurred.

The more direct your expression of remorse, the better. You don't have to grovel in shame, but all good apologies begin with this fundamental acknowledgment:

> "Hey, this is not right. I see that. I'm genuinely sorry about it."

If you lead with "If," and "But," or if you sneak in conditions and caveats, your apology will ring hollow. Take the hit, be sincere, and show that you're genuinely sad about the state of affairs, without overshadowing their feelings.

As far as is possible, use the words "I'm sorry" or "I apologize" without any hedging.

"I'm really sorry for the things I said this morning. That was wrong of me."

### **Say What Went Wrong**

**Give an explanation, not an excuse.**

Trust is broken. People's feelings are hurt. They might be wondering *why* the bad thing happened.

The next part of your apology helps provide the psychological closure of understanding exactly what went wrong—without veering into justifications that explain away your behavior.

Now's your chance to give context—not for your sake, but theirs. When someone wrongs us, it temporarily destabilizes our world. Sometimes it's easier for us to imagine that people are deliberately targeting us for a malicious attack, when the reality may be less black-and-white.

Put a clear label on the regrettable behavior *as they see it*. This means avoiding the dreaded, "I'm sorry you took things that way."

Provide a clear and simple explanation that doesn't put the blame on them. Help them understand the sequence of cause-and-effect, for example:

"I was feeling upset about work, and I lashed out at you."

## Take Full Responsibility

Immediately follow the above with a clear statement to show that you **take ownership of your behavior.**

Don't dilute it or soften it. Don't explain how bad your own behavior makes *you* feel, or how inconvenient it is for you to deal with the fallout now. Don't make this acceptance seem like a grand favor you're offering them, or that their grievance is mysterious or unreasonable: "Look, whatever's upset you, I'm sorry, OK?"

This part of the apology is very important, because the other person doesn't just need a "sorry", they need an "*I'm* sorry."

If possible, literally say the words, "I take responsibility." Variations include, "That's on me," or "It's my fault that happened."

To continue our example:

"That wasn't fair to you, and I take full responsibility for that."

## Say What You'll Do Differently
**Explain what happens now.**

You've apologized, you're genuinely remorseful, and you've owned the fact that the bad thing didn't just happen, but *you* made it happen. These are great first steps.

Stating how you plan to do better in future slightly shifts things and puts the focus on healing and growth. Guilt is good, but unless it inspires some sincere behavior change, it may feel kind of empty—especially if this behavior has happened before.

Reparations don't have to be big and formal, just show that you are actively considering what will change going forward:

"In the future, when I'm caught up in work like that, I'll make sure I cool off before I engage with you, so that I don't make the same mistake again."

## Ask How You Can Make It Right
**Make amends.**

If your actions have caused some obvious damage or harm, this is where you might offer to pay to have something replaced, or to make some small gesture to put things right. Be aware, though, that these actions themselves are not where the power of the apology lies—

your desire to *proactively restore the relationship* is what matters.

You can't undo the past. But you can take steps to make the future better. Importantly, this should be based on what the other person thinks would help them feel seen and heard—not what you think would.

"Is there anything I can do right to make this situation better?"

## **Ask for Forgiveness—But Only if It's Earned**
**Ask to be forgiven.**

Surprisingly, this is the least important part of your apology, despite it being the part that some people lead with. Asking outright for forgiveness may not be appropriate. This step is really for your benefit, not theirs, so don't be in too much of a rush to have your apology accepted if the other person isn't really there yet.

Ask gently, be brief, and then leave it.

Don't put conditions on anything, don't force anything, and don't put pressure on them to quickly absolve you and move on.

"Whenever you're ready, I hope you'll give me the chance to earn back your trust."

**Apology no-nos**

- Never expect praise or thanks for issuing an apology, no matter how high-minded you think you're being.
- Don't use your apology as an opportunity to share your own grievances about their behavior, or to sneakily redistribute the blame. "Well, we've *both* said some things we shouldn't have."
- Try to avoid "I feel really bad about what happened." It may be true, but for now it's irrelevant and may be perceived as a derail.
- Don't apologize if you sincerely don't think you're in the wrong. Tactical apologies often backfire and create resentment.
- "It was just a joke." "It didn't mean anything." "I don't know why I did that." Usually, phrases like this are simply not true. Be honest with yourself and with them. Take responsibility.
- Wherever possible apologize in person, as soon as possible after the incident. That said, don't force it on someone if they're not receptive; you may need to wait if emotions are high.
- Do not apologize for *their feelings*, but *your behaviors*.

An apology doesn't change what has happened, but it influences what can happen from this point on. Handle it correctly and an apology can be a doorway into better connection and more trust.

## Chapter 19. Offer Phony Empathy

The so-called "Golden Rule" has been with humanity a good few thousand years now: Treat others as you wish to be treated.

The principle is sound. If we wish to be treated with empathy and understanding, then we should understand that others want that too, and do our best to offer it to them.

The trouble is, there are more than 7 billion people on this planet. Do they all have precisely the same idea of what counts as "empathy" and "understanding"? Probably not.

We all have unique perspectives, values, experiences, goals, emotions, and communication styles. And that means that we all experience empathy in a slightly different way.

Take a look at the following three exchanges and see if you can spot what might be missing in each of them:

- A: "I'm feeling really left out of the group."
- B: "Oh don't worry, you're not! Everyone's welcome here."

- A: "I'm worried sick about my daughter."
- B: "Really? She's in her twenties, I'm sure she can take care of herself."

- A: "I keep second-guessing my decision… I just can't put my mind at ease about it."
- B: "I guess. You did what you could, though. No point dwelling on it, right?"

In their own way, each of these responses could be considered empathetic—yet they're not. The "Empathy Equation" can show us why.

## **The Empathy Equation**

### *WHAT + WHY + HOW*

This is the empathy equation by author and entrepreneur Greg Skloot, and it's about how to make our empathy more strategic, targeted, and sincere.

Before conversations, try to identify:

- WHAT does this person hope to gain from the conversation?
- WHY do they want that?
- HOW do they want to communicate with you?

***Real empathy***: The ability to understand and share the feelings and thoughts of another person.

***Fake empathy:*** The ability to understand our own feelings and thoughts about that person's feelings and thoughts.

It's a subtle—but major—difference that explains why so many superficially kind and supportive conversations actually feel hollow, weird, or uncomfortable. Have you ever opened up in a conversation only to feel a little *off* afterwards, as though you had been dismissed or shut down?

Chances are, it's because you were offered fake empathy, not the real deal.

**We need to talk to people in the way they want to be talked to.**

True empathy is not soft and fluffy—it's a smart and practical communication skill that helps you actually see into someone else's world. Nobody likes to think of themselves as *un*empathetic, but unless we are carefully considering what the other person actually wants and needs from the conversation, that's a risk we take.

Most of us are switched on enough to know that outright insensitivity is rude, but the truth is that it doesn't take much to create a feeling of dismissal or invalidation. Any time we subtly imply that someone's feelings don't really make sense to us, then the other person is unlikely to feel seen or heard, let alone supported.

## **Know WHAT the Other Person Needs from This Conversation**

Occasionally, people will talk just for the sake of talking, but most of the time, conversations happen because people are trying to get something they want from the interaction. Such as:

- Comfort and reassurance
- Advice
- Connection
- Solutions
- Clarity
- Agreement
- Praise
- Perspective
- Respect
- Acknowledgement
- Validation

It's always worth clearly understanding your own goals and agendas for a conversation. But don't stop there—ask yourself, "What do they want from this interaction?"

What we want and what they want might be two totally different things. Good communication means we can express what we want; **empathy means we're open and receptive to what *they* want.**

Consider this example again:

"I'm feeling really left out of the group."

What does this person want from having this conversation with you? Pause here and really think about it; if you were saying these words, what unspoken emotional need might *you* be expressing?

More than likely, this person is asking for their feelings to be acknowledged. It's as though they're offering up their perspective and experience and saying, "Here's what I see… do you see this, too?"

Looking at it this way, you can see why the response "Oh don't worry, you're not! Everyone's welcome here," will *not* feel good. It's dismissing the way the person feels.

Everyone may be technically welcome, but does that cancel out the fact that they don't feel this way? By responding like this, you are essentially saying to them, "You're mistaken."

Instead, a truly empathetic response might be: "Oh wow, I'm really sorry to hear that. Can you tell me a little more about what's made you feel this way?"

This response not only validates that the person has a right to feel this way, it also shows that you care for these feelings by inviting the person to elaborate.

## **Understand WHY That Need Matters to Them**

People have different personalities. Two people may want the same things but for entirely different reasons.

Once you've identified what a person is trying to gain from a conversation, ask yourself, "*Why* does this matter so much to them?"

Let's return to this example:

"I'm worried sick about my daughter."

The WHAT: This person may be looking for reassurance or support.

Now, what about the WHY?

Asking this question may reveal just how little you actually understand about the other person's situation. By jumping in to respond with "I'm sure she can take care of herself," we make the assumption that they're worried about their daughter's safety. What if they're actually worried about how the daughter's actions might affect others? What if they're worried about being held responsible for their daughter's choices?

Unless we know the WHY, our empathy is going to be pretty flimsy.

**When we barge in with assumptions from our own frame of reference, we make our empathy about us, not them**. Instead, we could say,

"That sounds difficult. What do you think you're most afraid will happen?"

Failed empathy often stems from us comparing the other person's perspective against our own and making a judgment on *that*.

- "That doesn't seem like such a big deal."
- "I don't get why this bothers you so much."
- "You're overreacting/being too sensitive."

Frankly, it doesn't really matter if something makes sense to us. We are not the ones it needs to make sense to! Instead, empathy means respecting that it *does* matter to others and trying to understand how and why.

"It seems like this means a lot to you. I'd feel the same if I were in your position." (Meaning, if something that mattered to me was under threat, I'd be upset too).

### **React HOW They Need You To**

Let's say your friend tells you, "I keep second-guessing my decision… I just can't put my mind at ease about it." They keep bringing the idea up, clearly wanting to talk. But HOW they want to talk matters.

Do they want…

- Tough love
- Gentle, kind support and handholding
- A "sounding board"
- An encouraging pep talk
- Someone to "think through" a problem with them
- A reality check
- Quiet presence and reflection
- A mix of several or all of these?

People may need a quick check-in or a meaty hour-long chat. They may prefer texts and emails, or they might need that face-to-face connection. They may need a lot all at once, or lots of little bits spread out.

The question to ask yourself is, **"How does this person want to receive my care, attention, and empathy?"**

It's not about the form of empathy that feels most natural, comfortable, or logical to *you*. It's about the form of empathy that will be best received and appreciated by *them*.

If someone craves rich, highly vulnerable emotion-talk that feels cathartic, then you show a lack of empathy if you respond to them with a cut-to-the-chase pep talk and "You got this, tiger."

At the same time, if someone needs clarity and practical support, you are not being empathetic by quietly bullying them into an emotionally exhausting therapy session with you. Take a look:

"I just need to grit my teeth and find a way to get through this." *(I need practical support.)*

- Fake empathy: "How are you feeling about it, though? Let's talk about it." *(I'm offering emotional support, whether you want it or not)*
- Real empathy: "I got you. So, what's the next step, as far as you see it? Anything I can help with?" *(I want to help you practically. Tell me how!)*

If we insist that empathy is only allowed to take on a form that we approve of, then we cut off our empathy at the root.

**Instead of asking what we would appreciate if we were in their position, we should ask what *they* would appreciate in *their* position. Big difference!**

Chapter 20. Compliment Selfishly

If you want to really mess up your conversations, fil them up with flattery, fawning, and cheap sweet talk.

A sincere compliment is like gold dust in a conversation.

An insincere one, on the other hand, is a kind of counterfeit currency—when you see it, you suspect some kind of transaction is underway!

- "Oh, I love your shoes!" (Translation: Let's center me and my good taste. Oh, and by the way, please look at *my* shoes and say how great they are, too!)
- "Wow, you're so good at that!" (Translation: Now could you do it for me...?)
- "You're such a kind person." (Translation: Please say yes to the request I'm about to make.)

Sincere compliments certainly exist. But if we're honest with ourselves, **compliments are sometimes *take* disguised as *give*.** When your compliment is more about you than it is about the person receiving it, then it's not really a compliment anymore. The person receiving it won't feel praised and appreciated—they'll feel slightly manipulated.

Compliments are like apologies in this regard; an insincere compliment is worse than nothing at all.

Here's why compliments can flop:

- They're vague, generic, and low effort ("Nice work!").

- They center the speaker ("I love it when women wear their hair down").

- They conceal a hidden agenda ("You're always so generous with gifts…").

- They feel untrustworthy and ego-driven ("You're a *genius*!").

A compliment can be well-meaning and still come across as shallow. Remember that when people hear a compliment, they're not just listening to what you're saying… they're listening to *why* you're saying it.

The truth: **Most people don't want compliments. They want acknowledgement.**

What's the difference? Let's explore.

### **Remove "I" to Stop Making It About You**

What's so bad about saying "I like your shoes," anyway?

Well, let's pick this apart. Perhaps you really *do* like them. But what does that mean, ultimately? You're pointing out something in the world you personally like. You unintentionally shift the focus to yourself—in particular, to your tastes, preferences, or values.

Now, this is subtle, but it matters. If my praise of somebody's shoes simply comes from my liking them, all I'm really saying is, "I approve of you" or even "I like the things I like." You're making your own taste the yardstick and measuring them against it. Not much of a compliment, right?

Instead, a sincere compliment should showcase and acknowledge the other person, in this case, *their* great fashion sense.

"You always put together such unique and beautiful outfits!"

This may look like a small tweak, but it makes a world of difference. "You did well," will always feel different to "I think you did well."

A compliment often comes with an agenda. But **acknowledgment is always about the other person, not you.**

## **Be Specific So the Praise Lands with Meaning**

In a way, generic compliments can almost feel like insults.

If someone tosses out a lackluster "Great job," without a second thought, chances are you won't genuinely feel as if your work has been noticed and appreciated. They're just ticking a box. Being polite. The result is a totally meaningless compliment that can actually create distance, not connection.

- "Did I really do a great job?"
- "What part of it was so great, anyway?"
- "Did they even pay attention to what I did, or are they just saying what they think I want to hear?"
- "Hang on, does this hollow-sounding compliment actually mean I did a poor job?!"

**Specificity shows effort.** It shows the other person that you are paying attention and that you care. You're not "being polite"—you're genuinely recognizing something of value in them and want them to know about it.

To stop compliments from feeling empty, get specific. Be clear about exactly what you're complimenting and why. Point out precisely how the world is better because of them. This specificity will inspire trust and feel really, really good for the recipient.

"You handled that difficult client with loads of patience and tact. You didn't just defuse the situation; you actually brought them round and forged a pretty good relationship there. Well done."

The deeper message: *I saw what you did, and it was good.*

## **Highlight What Your Praise Reveals About Their Strengths**

- "You're so pretty!"
- "That's such an interesting last name."
- "You have a great accent."

What do these compliments have in common?

Each of them praises a thing that the recipient doesn't actually have any control over. Being attractive or possessing a certain accent or last name are largely accidents of birth. In praising these things, we're essentially saying, "Good work for being lucky, I guess!"

Compliments like these will seldom register as especially meaningful. In fact, people who are routinely praised for things that are not in their control can feel a slight erosion of self-worth, especially if people are simultaneously ignoring all their hard-won accomplishments.

Compliments like this are ego-based. Instead, **try to understand what people value in themselves, and praise that**. Let your compliments reflect their own value systems and the efforts they make. When you reaffirm that you see people in the way that they'd like to see themselves, then your words will be felt as sincere recognition, not just flattery.

- What are their strengths?
- What are their values?
- What are their goals?
- What are most of their efforts aimed at?
- How do they think of their own accomplishments?

Try to target your compliment so that it puts all of the above front and center.

Just as with empathy, a compliment is only a good one if it's received that way.

**Bear in mind that what might feel like a compliment to one person won't necessarily feel like that to another.**

For example, it may be that someone is actually proud of their accent, because it sets them apart and reinforces a link with a cultural heritage they cherish. Complimenting their accent would feel like real recognition of their identity.

Or it may be that this person is tired of people lazily commenting on the most obvious fact about them—their accent—without taking the time to listen to what they're actually saying.

**How can you make sure that you're offering genuine praise and not superficial compliments?**

- Before you speak, think carefully about how your words may be received.
- Pay attention to what people themselves are highlighting as a source of pride or meaning—then reinforce that.
- Be mindful of your language. Compare "That's a nice dress," vs. "That dress makes you look good," vs. "You look good in that dress."
- Believe in your own compliments. If you don't believe your own words, chances are they won't, either!
- Be realistic. Hyperbole brings in elements of competition and comparison. Your compliment is not a prize they win, and it doesn't have to be over-the-top.
- Offer a compliment in a casual way that doesn't come with any obligation to respond in kind. Compliment, then move swiftly on.

**Things to avoid:**

- Making comments on physical appearance, especially when it comes to beauty or sex appeal—unless you're actually flirting!
- Making comments on money or possessions. Things can get awkward fast.
- Making accidental backhanded compliments. "Wow, this tastes surprisingly good."

**Flattery is shallow. Compliments are often one-dimensional. But real recognition and validation is about seeing someone in the way they want to be seen.**

Chapter 21. Listen… with the Intent to Reply

Hey, are you really listening?

Or are you just waiting patiently for your turn to talk?

**Listening to understand is not the same as listening to respond.**

When someone is merely listening to respond, you might not necessarily be able to put your finger on why it feels off, but you can feel it. They're quiet, they're nodding along, and they're smiling at all the right places, and yet it somehow doesn't feel like they're really there.

What's going on?

The *performance* of listening is not the same as listening.

Performance listening *looks* like genuine listening, but that's sort of the point. It's not coming from a genuine place of interest and care, but rather the intention is to give a passable appearance of interest and care.

Giving such a performance requires conscious effort—which takes us out of the moment and into our own heads. **If we're carefully thinking about what we'll say, or when and how we'll say it, we're simply no longer present.** We may miss all sorts of subtle emotional undercurrents, clumsily rush in to make statements that are slightly out of step with the other person, or accidentally derail the whole conversation.

Have you ever been talking to someone and they suddenly say something that applies to a part of the conversation that came and went five minutes ago?

You realize that they've not registered anything you've said in that five minutes, because they've been quietly rehearsing a response... and just waiting for you to stop talking so they could spring it on you!

How do you feel?

It doesn't matter how many "uh huhs" they threw your way or how much eye contact they made. It doesn't matter that if a gun were put to their head, they could probably recall the bare details of what you were saying.

*They weren't listening, and you knew it.* They were not focused on you and the living, breathing interaction underway, but rather their own agenda. You probably felt many things, but one thing you *didn't* feel was listened to.

**Signs you may be listening with an agenda:**

- You often feel a little impatient with people as they talk.

- You find yourself thinking, "Yes, yes, I get it," and zone out while they elaborate on a point you feel you've already understood.
- You sometimes quietly make a note of various "points" the speaker has made so you can go back and address each of them when it's your "turn".

If any of this sounds familiar, don't worry—most of us indulge in this habit now and then! Here's how to train yourself out of it and **have the conversation you're actually in.**

## Mirror Their Words Before Making Your Point

Slow down. Stop thinking of where the conversation is going (and where you want to steer it), and make sure you've properly covered the ground you're on right here and now.

Regularly repeat back what you've heard with little summaries and paraphrases.

- "So, what I'm hearing is…"
- "Just to confirm, the biggest problem as you see it is…"
- "So, it seems like…"

When you pause this way, you're demonstrating that you care more about properly understanding what they're saying, than barging in to get across what you want to say. People feel far more heard when you simply take the time to communicate, "I heard this. Is this what you meant?" before continuing.

## **Acknowledge the Emotion Before the Logic**

**Sometimes, we can be in a hurry to move emotions along to some kind of resolution.** This may come from a place of genuinely wanting to help, but it can come across as a desire to move on from emotions as fast as possible.

If someone has just shared their emotions with you, just be there for a moment with them, exactly where they are.

- No rush to make pronouncements about anything
- No pressure to fix, understand, or control
- No urgency to move on to the next thing

Mirroring people's words shows that we acknowledge the informational content they've shared.

It's also important that we also take a moment to recognize and accept the emotional content, too.

"You seem so overwhelmed. I'm sure this is really hard."

And that's all. No "but," No "and."

It may come down to advice eventually but remember that people can't accept your suggestions until they feel seen and understood first.

## **Stop Multitask Listening**

Of course you shouldn't be fiddling with your phone while someone talks to you, or slyly watching TV out the corner of one eye. But you don't need screens and smartphones to be distracted! If your attention is split *internally*, that matters too.

Be present and consciously choose to shelve any random thoughts till later. If this proves difficult, that's OK. Just be honest: "Hey, I'm sorry. This conversation really matters to be but I'm a bit distracted at the moment. Can we come back to this a little later so I can give you my full attention?"

## **Ask Clarifying Questions**

We've already seen that one of the best ways to show you're actually paying attention is to ask questions. Not any old questions, specifically **follow-up questions that meaningfully connect to what they've already said**. This does two things:

1. Shows that you are present and have heard their message
2. Shows that you are not busy preparing to launch into your own message

Pick up the thread of what they're saying and unravel it a little, see where it goes. Invite them to elaborate. Ask for details.

- "So, what happened next?"
- "Can you explain a little more what you meant by that part?"
- "Wait, so you're referring to today's meeting, not yesterday's?"

Show people that you're actually invested in what they're telling you. Value what you're hearing, and don't rush to assume that you already possess the full picture.

A single genuine request to understand more about what someone is going through is worth a dozen reflexive, lazy responses.

## **Get Feedback on How You Listen**

It's easy to believe that you are better at listening than you really are. But there is one surefire way to find out how good your listening skills really are, and what you could be doing to improve: ask.

Find someone you trust and explain that you're trying to be a better listener. If you want them to be honest and give you feedback you can really use, do your best not to argue back or get defensive. Just absorb it, thank them, and see what single thing you can do today that will start closing that gap.

You don't need to be this formal and serious about it, however. You can build in a natural request for feedback while you're having the conversation, especially if that conversation feels a little heated or volatile.

- "Hey, it feels like there might be some misunderstanding going on here. Can I ask you honestly, do you feel like I've properly understood you? I'm trying to learn to be better at listening."

Getting feedback on how you listen can also be a great way to signal a desire to reconnect *after* a disagreement or conflict.

- "I can see now that I wasn't really hearing you. I want to be a better listener, though. Any advice about how I can listen better in the future?"

Even if there isn't any advice forthcoming, a sincere gesture to improve shows real willingness and maturity.

Listening to someone is so much more than just understanding the idea they've communicated. When people feel listened to, they feel respected, they feel safe, and they feel valued.

There's no reason to give a performance, to rehearse a retort, or to rush to the next clever or useful thing we might say. People don't need that from us. What they do need is for us to be present enough to say, "I hear you," and mean it.

**Seek to understand before you seek to be understood.**

**Listen with the same enthusiasm with which you want to be heard.**

## Chapter 22. Run out of Things to Say

One way to kill a conversation is to let fear, judgment, assumption, and stale routine take over. But on the other extreme, conversations can go out with a whimper, as one or both parties simply run out of steam. The topic feels spent, the energy lulls and it's like the moment has come and gone.

Silence may result, but it's actually just a symptom. The real problem? Well, there isn't one.

The truth is that all conversations—even the really, really good ones—have a shelf life. Every dialogue has a beginning, middle, and end, and every interaction has peaks and valleys. Reaching a transition point in a conversation is *not* the end of the world if you know how to smoothly transition and re-engage with purpose.

Conversations are not static things—they *move*. And that means that **pacing, flow, and rhythm are important.**

Good conversations are a strange mix of relaxation and control. We need to hold on, but not too tightly.

It's a little like driving a stick shift. On any drive there are times you speed up and times you slow down. To keep going, you *need* to change gear now and then, or you risk stalling. In the same way, a conversation needs to be carefully steered if you hope to have a smooth ride.

First things first: **Don't fear the lull.**

Experienced drivers know that when the car's engine starts shuddering a little, it's a sign to gear down. There's no point freaking out about it, giving up, or assuming that you're doing something wrong. This engine shudder is just a helpful little sign that you need to switch things up to make a transition.

It's nothing to be afraid of.

Now and then, you may notice the engine of your conversation start to shudder and splutter a little. Don't panic! Just take it as a sign: You need to switch gear.

The "Open Loop" strategy is a fantastic tool to help you do just that. It's a communication tactic that lets you hold the conversation—but not too tightly. Essentially, the trick is to plant several little seeds called "open loops."

**An open loop is a new topic you raise but leave unresolved on purpose**. The idea is that if/when the conversation lulls, you can return to that topic seamlessly and keep your momentum.

An open loop is like a little seed that you plant. It's a backup plan, or a lifeline thread you can keep in the bank and pull out when the current thread has run its course. When done well, your conversation partner won't even know that you've done anything; they'll just enjoy what feels like the conversation's natural flow.

Have you ever ended a fantastic conversation where you got the feeling that there was still so much more that could have been said? That's the power of open loops. In the best possible way, **unfinished business of this kind makes a conversation feel lively, rich, and exciting.** Rather than feeling like you're in a dry desert scrambling for *something* to say, you create the feeling of conversational abundance and possibility.

The conversation doesn't feel forced or difficult. It feels infinite.

Learning to use the open loop strategy does take a little skill, though, just like driving stick. Here's how.

## **Open, Don't Conclude**

In school, you may have been taught to create logical, neatly structured essays that clearly outlined a point from start to finish and kept fluff and tangents to a minimum. Conversations, however, are nothing like essays. In fact, a good conversation is often a big mess!

Try to resist the natural urge to *close* loops. It may feel weird at first to deliberately leave some threads dangling and unresolved, but this is creating possibility.

One way to create an open loop is to simply change track halfway through a story, instead of diligently telling the complete tale from start to finish. Sticking to one topic at a time may feel satisfying in the moment, but what about when you get to the end of that story? You could be left high and dry with an awkward kind of "now what?" energy.

Instead, **embrace the mess and deliberately go off on tangents**.

- Dead conversations: linear, closed, and final
- Lively conversations: layered, branching, and flexible

Here's how that looks:

You say, "We all decided to do something a little different for Christmas last year, and we booked an all-inclusive trip to Mexico, man was that a weird week! Have you ever been, by the way? To Mexico?"

Initially, you launch what looks like it will be a story about that time you spent Christmas in Mexico. But suddenly, you go off on a tangent and ask if they've ever been to Mexico.

Just like that, there are *two* conversation topics on the table. You've left the Christmas anecdote open and unresolved, and it's there ready and waiting for you when/if the Mexico thread runs dry.

The longer the conversation goes on, the more loops you open. The more seeds you plant, the more possibilities you have for future harvests. In James P. Carse's book *Finite and Infinite Games*, he explains that a finite "game" is played for the purpose of winning, but an infinite game for the purpose of *continuing the game play.*

Good conversations feel infinite. Open loops are how you create that expansiveness.

In other words, don't be in too much of a hurry to wrap things up. Be playful, keep things open, and understand that the enjoyment of a story is not in its completion, but in its unfolding.

**It's not chaos—it's play and possibility.**

## **Transition With Intention**

The engine is shuddering. Time to change gear. But not just any gear will do!

You need to switch in a meaningful, deliberate way. If the transition feels forced and unnatural, it won't work. It's like gearing up when you should gear down, or trying to shift into fifth when you're still in second.

Let's say you started telling your Christmas in Mexico story, but you left it as an open loop and asked about whether they'd been to Mexico. Let's say they had, and you then had a five-minute conversation about Mexican food, and tequila. They share a cute little anecdote about tequila, but once their story's told, there's a lull.

Now's your chance.

You go back to the Christmas story and pick up exactly where you left off:

"So anyway, we were in this all-inclusive resort—really nice place—and we'd booked it for the week…"

Here you can open more loops. Or you can deliberately link back this story to a previous loop: "Funny you should mention that thing about tequila, by the way, because that very evening they had a tequila tasting thing in the lobby. I didn't go, but my friend did—that's a whole separate story! But anyway, it was Christmas eve, and there we all were..."

The more loops you have open, the more options you have for making thoughtful shifts and transitions. It will feel easy and comfortable to circle back to one of the many open threads on the table.

**A few warnings, however:**

- **It's not an open loop if you've already concluded the main storyline.** Returning to a *closed* loop will feel forced and a bit lame. For example, if you've told your Mexican Christmas story to the end, don't return to it again. It's done.
- **Try to return to an open loop just once, then consider it spent**. Long-running in jokes and "call backs" can certainly create a feeling of rapport and connection, but they need to be co-creations—don't keep returning to the same old loop over and over or it'll start to feel weird.
- **Try to find some thematic connection between the old loop and the new,** if possible, so the transition doesn't feel too abrupt.

- **Just because you open a loop, it doesn't mean you *have to* return to it.** It's just there as your insurance policy.
- **There's no need to return to a loop if the current thread is alive and well.** Jump ship when a topic starts to fail or slightly before, but if you abandon a topic while the other person is still enjoying it, the conversation may start to feel fragmented.

One great way to open loops is with questions that deliberately shift attention to the other person.

- If you mention Mexico, you could pause and say, "Have you ever been?"
- If you mention something about tequila, you might stop and say, "Are you a fan, by the way?"
- And if you're describing what your friend does for work, you might quickly say, "That reminds me, I wanted to ask what you did for work…?"

Roping people in this way keeps things lively but it also prevents your story from feeling like a shapeless monologue. If you have the good fortune of finding yourself chatting to a skilled conversationalist, asking questions gives them an opportunity to open up loops of their own.

## **Return When Energy Dips**

How do you know when to go back to an open loop?

Sometimes, it's not necessarily that there isn't more to say on a particular topic, but rather that you have reached the end of people's attention, and willingness to stay focused on that topic.

You can be talking about the most fascinating topic in the world, but **if people's energy is dropping and their interest isn't there, then it's time to move on.**

You can instantly pep up flagging attention with little hints and cues that suggest that the conversation is about to take a new turn. Certain phrases announce a conversational gear shift, and act like a little breath of fresh air:

- "Oh, that reminds me…"
- "Speaking of earlier, I never finished telling you about…"
- "Funny you should mention that, because…"
- "That makes me think of…"
- "Anyway, I've been meaning to tell you…"

**You can also create a feeling of anticipation by deliberately hinting at *future* open**

**loops**. Suggesting that some interesting ground may be covered at some point in the near future creates a sense of enjoyable expectation. People sit up and pay closer attention—when will the future loop arrive?

Try:

- "Oh, you're going to laugh when I tell you in just a minute..."
- "You won't believe what happened to me yesterday; but first, tell me your news."
- "When we both know each other little better I'll tell you my Mexico story..."

Little conversational cliffhangers like this create a feeling of hopeful suspense. Rather than dreading the silences and the burden of filling them, there's something fun to look forward to. Especially in a flirtatious context, this can be a powerful way to stir up good chemistry.

Once you master open loops in conversation, you may even notice how some loops can be carried over *between* conversations. When you hear someone say something interesting in passing, grab a hold of it and file it away mentally for use later on. The next time you meet for conversation, for example, you can kick off immediately with this open loop, "Hey, did I hear you mention that you had signed up for the marathon this summer? Is that this weekend?"

In just a few seconds, you've confidently launched a new conversation, demonstrated your interest and attention, and created a comfortable sense of being "in the loop" with one another. Open loops not only help you create conversations that feel full and engaging, but they'll help you foster deeper and more meaningful connections with people over time.

**The brain craves closure. When you deliberately interfere with this impulse, you stimulate curiosity, bring in fresh energy, and create a sense of anticipation—the subtle feeling that there's more to come.**

Chapter 23. Pretend to Agree with Someone

A really effective way to completely tank a conversation is to smile politely and agree with everything you hear. Yes, really!

Where did we get the idea that disagreement is dangerous? Being polite is one thing, but many of us quietly suffer under the assumption that if we want to get along and have people like us, the only way to do it is to *agree* with them.

We call this keeping the peace or avoiding conflict. We think we're being nice.

But pause for a moment and consider how nice it really is to *fake* agreement. Imagine for a moment that you have just had a pleasant interaction with someone, only to be told afterwards that the other person was faking it, and the sense of harmony you felt was just an act.

Doesn't feel especially *nice* of them, right?

**The truth is that fake agreements don't protect a relationship. It cheapens it.**

Pretending to agree is trading off honesty for (temporary) harmony. We silence our own views, opinions, and values for the other person's sake, and to spare ourselves potential discomfort and awkwardness.

But is it worth it?

If you have any relationships in your life right now that are built on faux agreement, you already know how much resentment, exhaustion and distance it can create. Maintained over the long term, such relationships can even spur an identity crisis. If nobody really knows what you really think, you can start to lose touch with that yourself.

The pretend agreement habit can sneak up on some of us.

- Maybe we're people-pleasers and hold the unconscious belief that the cost of connection is for us to sacrifice a little of who we really are.
- Maybe we're anxious or afraid of being rejected.
- Maybe we've just let genuine cordiality get out of hand.

If you're still not convinced, consider this: **Fake agreement can actually *increase* discord and hostility in the long term, not prevent it.** Why? You sense a moment of disagreement, and swallow it down, nodding and smiling instead. But this creates a kind of conversational imbalance. You may almost feel like you've done them a favor.

You've avoided confrontation, but at what cost?

You've created a little distance.

You've introduced a small bit of tension.

You've brought in a tiny splinter of resentment.

Over time, this is precisely the sort of thing that chips away at *real* harmony and connection over time. You hold back your real thoughts and bite your tongue… but then one day you explode and say something far more destructive. And what good is that?

The irony is that if you truly value connection and cohesion, one of the best things you can do is be *genuine*.

**It's not that disagreement is bad and agreement is good. Rather, it's about accepting that disagreement is a natural part of conversation and learning to navigate it well.**

Below are some ways to do just that, but before we explore them (how's that for an open loop?) let's quickly shatter some conversational myths once and for all. Here are the myths:

- Keeping your real feelings to yourself is the safest option.

- Your opinion is not special or valuable anyway.
- You ultimately don't have any real say in how the conversation goes, and your input is irrelevant.
- Either you agree and go along, or you lose.

Let's reframe these:

- Inauthenticity is often the riskiest move you can make.
- You have an obligation to bring to the table the things that only you can bring.
- Your voice matters, and your input can change things.
- Disagreement doesn't threaten connection—in fact, sometimes it deepens it.

In real life, people form rich, complex, and meaningful bonds with *human beings*—not with smiling yes-men who have no strong feelings. Fakeness is not a gift or a favor. It's not nice. It's a cop out.

**Instead, show up fully in conversations as the person you are. Differences and disagreements are not problems until you make them one.** Now, to close that loop:

## Validate Before You Disagree

Bite your tongue, or cause offense?

Say what you really think, or have some peace and quiet?

Actually, it doesn't have to be either/or. Think about it: Why should we be uncomfortable with disagreement? The world is a big place, and no two people are identical. Is it really so unthinkable that occasionally we won't gel with our conversation partners?

The first thing is to get clear within ourselves how we want to think of discord and difference. If we are secure in ourselves with who we are, we no longer need to frame things in terms of threat, loss, or discomfort. Disagreements just become an unremarkable fact of life... or perhaps even a source of interest and enjoyment.

Our approach and attitude make the difference:

- **Passive** means we roll over, concede, and submit. We erase ourselves.
- **Aggressive** means we dominate and push our agenda. We attempt to erase others so we can amplify ourselves.

However, these are not our only options. There is a third possibility:

- **Assertive** means we comfortably own and express our views. We don't erase ourselves nor seek to erase others.

This can be a bit of an "Aha!" moment. Our view can exist *alongside* their view. No competition, no conflict.

Assertive language is warm, firm, and respectful. A great way to strike a balance is to affirm and acknowledge their position first, and then do the same for yours.

- "I hear you, and that's a god point. I have a different opinion, though."
- "I understand where you're coming from. It definitely makes sense. As for me, I see things another way."
- "You've articulated that really well. Even still, I'm not sure we're on the same page with that one."
- "You know, that's a really interesting perspective. I hadn't thought about it like that before. But I don't think I agree."

Honestly and respectfully acknowledging differences is not a declaration of war. You can still talk, you can still connect, and you can still enjoy and learn from one another.

(Quick tip: Try to avoid "You're entitled to your opinion." They are, but not because you graciously granted it.)

## **Get Comfortable Being Uncomfortable**

Many of us have been conditioned by past experiences to resist and flee anything that looks like conflict, discomfort, or tension. Often, for very good reason!

We may have been taught that every disagreement is a battle, and that there can only be one winner. We don't want to fight, and we certainly don't want to lose, so we make a quite understandable concession and try to wriggle out of the whole thing entirely.

But let's take a closer look at those underlying assumptions.

At any time, you are at total liberty to choose not to "fight." In fact, you don't have to use the war mindset at all, if you don't want to. **A disagreement does *not* compel a response, require you to choose sides, or force a win/lose conclusion.** You don't need to prevent the war out there by starting a war inside yourself.

There doesn't have to be a war in the first place.

That's a frame some people have. But it doesn't have to be *your* frame.

You can simply... do nothing. You don't have to agree *or* disagree. You can just acknowledge that there's a difference and bow out gracefully.

Of course, sometimes disagreements do morph into conflicts, but remind yourself that you can always decide to prioritize connection and harmony *even in the midst of disagreement*. And this is the mindset shift that relieves anxiety the most: **You do not have to agree with someone in order to cooperate well with them.**

## Say No Without a Speech

Dig deep into the roots of conflict avoidance and people-pleasing, and you may find a faulty assumption: It's somehow up to you to get everyone alongside you.

Perhaps you've absorbed the idea that you are only allowed to have your own opinion and perspective if you can defend it adequately, justify it, explain it, or otherwise sell it to someone who thinks something different.

Let yourself off the hook. You don't owe anyone this. **You can say no to something without getting other people's permission or approval first**. Even if other people may not like it, your no stands just the same.

Be neat, clean, and to the point. "I'm going to have to disagree with you on that one!"

There's no need for drama. You have nothing to feel guilty or awkward about. Deliver the fact of your disagreement like you'd deliver any other neutral fact about yourself.

"I have blue eyes."

You don't need to give a full-length TED talk about why it's OK for you to have blue eyes. You just do, now let's move on.

The magic happens when you realize that on the other side of a clear, respectful expression of disagreement lies a whole vista of potential connection. It may sound strange, but even conflicts and tensions can bring people closer together, if they're real.

Don't fake your way through life. Speak up. It's a relief when you realize that you don't have to be afraid of difference—in yourself or others. In fact, handled well, differences are precisely what adds color, depth, and meaning to life.

People-pleasing, fear, and conflict aversion is: "I'm agreeing because I'm afraid of what will happen if I don't."

*This is not harmony. It's fear, transaction, loss aversion, and obligation.*

**Real kindness and connection: "Agree or disagree, I choose to respect you and protect our connection."**

**This is real harmony.**

Chapter 24. Never. Stop. Talking.

You know when you open a YouTube video hoping for a quick answer to a question you have, but the presenter insists on blabbing aimlessly for the first twelve and a half minutes?

Well, one way to really wreck your own real-life relationships is to forget you're in a conversation at all and subject the other person to the same sort of thing.

Maybe you're in a conversation when someone's eyes start to glaze over and you suddenly realize you've been monologuing for five minutes straight. Yup. Embarrassing. Welcome to the Overtalking Olympics, where you're currently winning the gold medal!

But don't worry—overtalking is pretty common. Most people don't set out to be over-talkers. It just happens by accident.

The cruel irony is that we can slip into verbal diarrhea precisely because we're nervous, anxious, or insecure about our contribution to the conversation. Maybe we're just excited. Either way, taking too long a turn in conversation can steamroll the natural shape of the dialogue and leave everyone—including us! —feeling exhausted.

Overtalking is fun in the moment, but it's not worth it:

- You bore people
- You wear out their politeness
- You shatter any sense of your own mystery
- You start sounding like a teacher or a preacher (and who listens to them?!)
- You risk coming across as arrogant
- You miss out on all the interesting stuff they could be telling *you*!

Overtalking doesn't mean you're a bad person or a conversational narcissist. It's a habit anyone can fall into, but it's also a habit you can break. Here's how to rein it in.

### **Use the Traffic Light Rule**

Be time aware.

The "traffic light rule" can help:

**For the first 30 seconds, you've got the green light.** Talk away.

**After 30 seconds the yellow light goes on.** Keep tabs on where your listener is. If they look bored to tears and are longingly gazing at the door, stop talking. Pause to let them get a word in or bow out gracefully with a question for best results.

Even if they *do* look interested, however…

**By the time you hit 60 seconds, that's the red light: Wrap it up no matter what.**

If your listener is positively begging for you to go on after 60 seconds, then that's great. But allow yourself to be humbled by the fact that they probably won't be!

It's hard to know exactly how long 30 or 60 seconds are during a conversation, but you can train your internal clock by practicing alone with a timer. Imagine that someone has just asked you a question you're really going to enjoy answering. Set the timer and go—imagine talking as you would during a conversation.

A full minute is *a lot* of time, but it's also very easy to lose track of if you're not careful.

### Try a Silence Practice

Being a chatterbox may just be a part of your personality, but it's also a learned habit—which means you can unlearn it. Rather than framing this un-learning as a process where you *lose* something, think of it in terms of what you gain. Quietness brings wonderful things to conversations:

- Peace
- Relaxation
- Clarity
- Trust

- Ease
- Flow
- Potential

To Chatty Cathys, silence can just feel boring. Like a waystation you pass through en route to something you actually care about. But you can gently challenge this belief by deliberately being silent in everyday ways.

It's up to you how you do this, but here are some ideas:

- Go for a whole hour (or day, even) on mute.
- During a social gathering, give yourself little micro challenges, like only offering a sentence every ten minutes.
- When asked a question, force yourself to pause for a full 3 seconds before answering.

In time, you'll realize that **the goal isn't actually to talk less... it's to talk *better*.** With these practices, you train yourself to notice just how often you repeat yourself or speak carelessly or without any real control or precision. You may realize that there is an art and *discipline* to conscientious speech.

When you have a speech budget, you're encouraged to be more mindful about exactly how you're using your words. In real life, there really *is* a budget—people's attention spans are not infinite, nor do we have an eternity to explain what we mean.

**Be aware of how you use time, space, words, and attention. Aim for quality, not quantity.**

### Ask Yourself: "Is This for Me or for Them?"

With practice, you'll begin to notice yourself in conversations. Notice when you "have the floor." Pay attention to what you're saying, how you're saying it, and how long you're taking. Ask yourself internally:

- "Am I actually adding value here?"
- "Am I contributing, or am I just venting for my own relief or enjoyment?"
- "Is this still a conversation or am I making it a monologue?"

Overtalking can even lead to oversharing and other awkwardness. Instead, save it for your journal or therapist, and consciously choose to hand the reins over to the other person:

"Anyway, what do you think?"

### The Curse of the Overtalker

There can be many complex reasons behind overtalking.

- You feel compelled to impress or entertain, perhaps out of a sense of responsibility for maintaining the conversation alone.
- You mistakenly assume that because you're interested in what you're saying, that other people will be, too.
- You're not all that clear on what it is you're trying to say, and you're using talk to find your way out of your own muddled thoughts.

**Whatever the reason, though, overtalking tends to have the same effect on listeners: *They eventually stop listening.*** And when they do, we may find ourselves talking even more to recapture their flagging attention. This is the curse of overtalking.

And the way out is to simply be more mindful:

- Is it really only up to me to say interesting or entertaining things?
- Is this other person likely to be interested in what I want to tell them?
- Do I actually need to say anything here? Or have I already expressed it sufficiently?

Your contribution to a conversation can be thought of as a neat little package, with a beginning and end. Try to notice where the end is, and don't keep pushing past it.. Speak, then stop.

Trust that you've expressed yourself enough, and trust that other people have heard you. If you can practice a little restraint, you may discover that people do in fact hear and understand you without enormous efforts on your part.

Relax. Let things unfold. Conversation is a ping-pong game, and you can safely let the ball go. It will come back!

**It's better to say a little less and leave people curious, than say too much and leave them exhausted.**

**Be brief. Be brilliant. Be gone.**

Chapter 25. Forget to Make Introductions

It may seem strange to include a chapter about introductions at the very *end* of a book, but that's just it... failing to introduce yourself properly at the right time can indeed create awkwardness.

Maybe you were so intent on nailing those first few crucial moments of small talk that you breezed right past the introductions... and now you realize you don't know their name. Oops.

Or, maybe you're in a casual situation and people are drifting in and out of the group, but not everybody knows each other, so you're left clumsily smiling at someone, not quite sure who they are or how they fit into things.

In the past, etiquette mattered much more than it does today. However, our great grandparents went out of their way to observe social rules not to make their lives harder and more complicated, but to make them *easier*. The fact is that certain social niceties exist to grease the social machine and cut down on misunderstandings, upsets, and awkwardness. A proper introduction is just such a social nicety.

**There are two broad types:**

- Introducing yourself

- Introducing others

Understanding the unspoken rules around both is not just a matter of simple courtesy—it's a strategic and invaluable communication skill that shows others that you care about maintaining rapport.

So, what's the best way to take control of introductions?

## **Confidently Introduce Yourself When No One Else Does**

Even in formal or professional situations, you cannot always rely on other people to properly introduce you into a group. However, if you take the initiative to do it yourself, you dissolve any possible lingering tension, balance out the social dynamic, and send everyone a clear message: *I'm friendly, confident, and I'm not doing any of this on autopilot.*

**An introduction doesn't have to be clever or complex. It just needs to be clear and proactive.**

"Hi, I'm [name], it's nice to meet you."

It's a small thing that completely changes the feel of any conversation, whether casual or professional. You show that you're paying respectful attention, and that you expect the same in return.

If the situation is rather relaxed, simply saying "I'm [name], by the way" and extending your hand for a handshake will cover most bases. Be warm, relaxed, and open. Smile and make eye contact and, almost always, the other person will follow suit.

For those who stress about small talk and what to say, an introduction is really the lowest hanging fruit. It takes zero effort or originality, but instantly conveys trustworthiness and confidence. For maximum effectiveness, try to use your introduction as a segue into something else:

- Comment on the reason you're here right now. ("Hi I'm [name]. Are you guys buying tickets for the concert, too?")
- Comment on the thing that might link you together. ("Hi I'm [name]. I think we're both friends of the groom.")
- Ask a friendly question. ("Hi I'm [name]. Weird question, but can I ask where you bought that amazing bag from?")

## **Use the "What, So What, Now What" Framework**

What about professional contexts though? Perhaps you find yourself at a conference filled with strangers, or you're in a meeting where the host has uttered those chilling words:

"Let's quickly go around the table and introduce ourselves…"

In work contexts, it's usually not enough to just state your name. If you wish to stand out and be memorable in some way, a good professional introduction will act almost like a mini-resume or calling card.

One way to introduce yourself in a comfortable, seamless way is to follow a formula:

- **What**: State who you are and your role.
- **So What:** Briefly talk about what excites you or what you're currently interested in.
- **Now What:** Ask the other person a thoughtful question.

As an example: "Hi, I'm [name]. I work as a brand manager for a sustainable fashion label. I'm really interested in the growing trends around underconsumption, especially for younger demographics. What brings you to this conference?"

This format is short and sweet but gives the other person plenty to run with. They can respond in a number of ways to your expressed interests, they can answer your question, or they can take the opportunity to introduce themselves.

Either way, a few handy loops are opened and within a few quick seconds the ice will be broken.

If you're not used to delivering such an introduction, it can feel a little awkward at first. So practice. Jot down a few notes and variations, and teak the format a little before heading into every new situation or work event. If you have a ready-to-go introduction at hand, you'll feel far more comfortable and confident.

## **Always Introduce Others When You're the Common Link**

Imagine Emma is at a social gathering and talking to some acquaintances. A friend of Emma's approaches and begins to talk to her—but only to her. The acquaintances, who don't know Emma's friend, stand around uncomfortably while the friend proceeds to have a conversation with Emma about a topic that only him and Emma know about.

Emma turns away from the acquaintances to talk to her friend for a few minutes, but eventually picks the conversation with the acquaintances back up again. Now it's the friend's turn to stand around awkwardly. Since he's only catching the tail end of the conversation, he can't quite contribute. So he just stands there, silent.

*What's wrong with this picture?*

In fact, both Emma and her friend have committed a social faux pas. The friend has rudely butted into a conversation without introducing himself, and Emma has failed to properly introduce him and integrate him into the existing conversation.

The rule goes like this: **If someone joins a conversation where you know both parties involved, the onus is on you to introduce them to one another.** If you don't, you may end up with the weird standoff described above. Even if people do manage to eke out some chit chat in this situation, it's going to be pretty uncomfortable.

Instead, be polite and take a few moments to make everyone feel seen, included, and welcome. Provide context and structure for those important early moments and set the interaction off to a good start.

In this example, the friend could have led with an introduction:

"Oh, hey everyone, sorry to interrupt! I'm [name], I'm Emma's friend. We're on the same shift at work. Emma, could I have a quick word with you…?"

Note the simple format: [who you are] + [how you fit].

In this case, if the friend wants to have a private conversation with Emma, then it's best to signal this, rather than just launch into a conversation that others cannot participate in.

On the other hand, Emma could have seen her friend approaching and taken the initiative to quickly introduce him to everyone else.

"Everyone, this is [friend]! He's great. [Friend] have you met [acquaintances]? They're on the morning shift; you might not have seen them around. We were just talking about DNA ancestry tests. Have you ever done one of those, [Friend]?"

In just a few lines, Emma introduces everyone, explains existing relationships and connections, and offers a quick recap of where the conversation currently stands—so that the friend can comfortably join in. This way, nobody is being excluded or left hanging.

While this situation may seem quite specific, it's far more common than many of us realize. If you've ever been to a party or get-together that felt boring, stilted, or awkward, part of the reason could be that the host simply neglected to make proper introductions.

Without really knowing why, some people might be left feeling confused or unimportant, as though they are not officially included in the group. ("Who are all these people? How do they know each other? Am I the outsider here?")

Unknown variables in social interactions are stressful. Spare other people the burden and go out of your way to acknowledge them and, if they fail to return the favor, it's no problem; simply introduce yourself.

"I'm sorry, where are my manners? I'm [name]."

**Remember that civility costs little but buys much. Take charge, announce yourself with confidence, and take care to put others at ease.**

## Conclusion

Way back in the Introduction, we encountered a list of reasons that people yearn for connection. They may have been the exact reasons you decided to pick up this book:

- We want to feel seen and heard
- We want confirmation that we a part of something bigger than ourselves
- We want to be accepted for who we really are
- We want people to really *get* us
- We want to feel like our contributions matter and have value
- We want to feel like our perspective belongs and make sense

A fundamental mindset shift occurs when we understand that in conversation, *other people seek the very same things from us.*

To be masterful conversationalists, then, we need to invert the above:

- Make our conversation partner feel seen and heard
- Invite them to take part in something bigger
- Accept them for who they really are
- Do whatever you can to understand them
- Consider their contributions valuable

- Make room for and validate their perspective

Until you can say that you know how to approach people with *this* mindset, then you will always be a novice conversationalist.

Conversation fills a human need. Speak to this need and you'll elevate every conversation, whether it's a deep and meaningful conversation with a life partner or just chit chat at the bus stop.

1. Be present, listen, and absorb.
2. Don't just ask questions, be genuinely curious.
3. Embrace silence and pauses.
4. LISTEN.
5. Relax. Pace yourself. End things end when they're finished.
6. Be prepared but be open—hold the flow but not too tightly!
7. See people as friends, not adversaries.
8. Lead with cooperation, not competition.
9. Embrace care and compassion, not fear and defensiveness.
10. Open up and expand, don't contract and shut down.
11. Favor exploration, not control.
12. Prioritize connection above *everything*—including your own ego.

13. Don't give advice, lectures or stories—give presence.
14. Don't be boring. Don't be judgy. Don't be fake-nice.
15. Be mindful, be intentional, and take charge.

Oh—and don't forget to introduce yourself!

A conversation dies just like any other living things dies—it becomes old and tired and stiff and stale; it withers from neglect; maybe it's even murdered outright.

But a healthy conversation is a *living* thing.

It's dynamic, flexible, and playful.

When you sincerely believe that other people are fascinating, worthy, and more than deserving of your respectful attention, then everything clicks into place. Your conversations *come to life.*

Fortunately, the most exciting and satisfying conversations are still to come—so go out there and make them happen!

www.ingramcontent.com/pod-product-compliance
Lightning Source LLC
Chambersburg PA
CBHW060555080526
44585CB00013B/578